H[...]
YOU MUST WRITE A BOOK

STOP TRYING SO F*CKING HARD

LIVE AUTHENTICALLY, DESIGN A LIFE YOU LOVE, AND BE HAPPY (FINALLY)

ALSO BY HONORÉE CORDER

*Business Dating: Applying Relationship Rules in
Business for Ultimate Success*

*Tall Order: Organize Your Life and
Double Your Success in Half the Time*

*Vision to Reality: How Short Term Massive Action
Equals Long Term Maximum Results*

*You MUST Write a Book: Boost Your Brand,
Get More Business, and Become the Go-To Expert*

*I Must Write MY Book: The Companion Workbook to
You MUST Write a Book*

The Miracle Morning book series

The Prosperous Writer book series

The Successful Single Mom book series

The Write (Publish and Market) Like a Boss book series

*The Divorced Phoenix: Rising from the
Ashes of a Broken Marriage*

*If Divorce is a Game, These are the Rules: 8 Rules for
Thriving Before, During and After Divorce*

STOP TRYING
SO F*CKING HARD

Live Authentically,
Design a Life You Love,
and Be Happy (Finally)!

HONORÉE CORDER

Digital ISBN: 978-1-947665-07-1
Tradepaper ISBN: 978-1-947665-06-4

Cover: Dino Marino
Interior Design: Christina Gorchos

SPECIAL INVITATION

Be sure to grab two free chapters of my book on business networking:

HONOREECORDER.COM/BUSINESSDATING.

You can connect with me personally on Twitter @Honoree, or on Facebook.com/Honoree. Thank you so much for your most precious resource, your time. I look forward to connecting and hearing about your success soon!

TABLE OF CONTENTS

INTRODUCTION

IT'S TIME FOR YOU TO STOP TRYING SO FUCKING HARD.

If you have been struggling with self-doubt, anxiety, being discouraged, indecision, comparison-itis, exhaustion, promising too much, copious amounts of stress, worry, even profound sadness—or any other number of hard-as-fuck internal challenges, the time has come for you to stop.

Breathe.

And sit down to read this book.

Before I dive into the reason for this book and the content I know can help you, I want you to know I struggled with the use of the "not safe for work" word *fuck.*

I know you can't un-ring a bell, and some people just don't like swearing. Perhaps you're offended by my saucy language, and if you are, I hope you can look past it to get to my message. My desired outcome for this book is for every reader to take something powerful and positive from it and live their lives in a way that makes their heart sing.

So, if necessary, I apologize for my saucy language. But I mean, seriously, how else was I going to get your attention?

I didn't know another way to break your trance long enough to tell you something I know you have wanted—and needed—to hear:

You are enough. Right now. Just as you are. In your current state of being. It's time you enjoy the ride while you continue to grow as a person, discover your best self, and love (almost) every minute of your life.

Now that I do have your attention, it's vital for you to realize your actual problem: *you're trying too fucking hard.*

Did you know you can stop running like you're being chased by the ball, Indiana Jones? You can, and dare I say you must! You can drop the hammer you've been beating yourself over the head with, take your foot off the gas, and gain a new perspective—one that permits you to live life on your own terms, in a way that makes you feel so happy you can hardly stand it. So joyful that nothing can get a smile off of your face. Like a kid with a secret who's up to no good, except it's you, there's no secret, and you're giddy with good.

I've watched, for far too long, people around me getting in their own way. They are failing to achieve not only their dreams but even a basic level of daily happiness. They feel not enough—not smart enough, educated enough, powerful enough—not enough of whatever it is they think they need to be. They constantly berate themselves and engage in a variety of self-destructive behaviors to try to achieve an ideal that simply doesn't exist.

Have you bought books, attended courses or seminars, and then feel like a failure because you haven't achieved what others seemingly have achieved? Do you envy the "perfect lives" you see (according to social media)?

If you're like most, you strain and strive and hustle and compare, feeling inadequate, incapable, and exhausted.

I'm exhausted just writing that.

So again, I say stop. Breathe. And allow me to show you a more natural, less stressful, and more effective way of living. You can live in a world where you are validated by yourself, make decisions based on what you want and what brings you joy, and be successful—authentically successful—and ultimately happier than you've ever been.

When you let go of the need for external validation and cloak yourself in self-love and appreciation while you pursue a life that makes you blissfully happy, the sky then truly becomes the limit.

I want you to shine your light, which will permit others to shine theirs. When you're ready, let's begin.

Chapter One

YOU'RE TRYING TOO F*CKING HARD!

Give up being perfect for being authentic.

–HAL ELROD, Author, *The Miracle Morning*

THE FIRST STEP IN A LIFETIME OF HAPPINESS AND SUCCESS is taking a deep breath, followed by the realization that being yourself is easy.

It's being someone else, what most therapists call "the representative," well, that's exhausting.

The representative is the person you're sending out into the world via social media, on dates, to work, and to other social gatherings. You're dressing her up so she looks skinny, rich, and happy. You're posting selfies of her at the right angle, in perfect lighting, with the best filter to appear as though everything is hunky and/or dory. When, in fact, you might feel everything but … You're buying him the right car and living in the right neighborhood, so that others will approve. You're modeling his business, trying to *be him* so you can feel, just for one moment, a flash of happiness. What you think *he feels*.

What if, for just a moment, you told the representative to fuck right off and just started saying what *you* want to say, doing what *you* want to do, and going where *you* want to go?

You could wear what you want to wear, live where you want to live, and drive what you want to drive. Not because those things are socially, professionally, religiously (or any other "-ly") acceptable, but simply because doing so would make you feel downright blissful.

Today one of my inner-circle friends said to me, "You've got it all together. The rest of us merely appear that way."

She's right. Here's why:

I don't live two lives: what I post on social media and my reality are the same. What you see is what you get. I decided a long time ago that sending a representative out into the world (physically and on social media) was too tiring for me, and I chose to be myself. All the time.

It's true I don't post my personal business on social media. I have as many challenges as the next person (I'm human, after all). I don't need others to send me virtual hugs, just as I don't need lots of likes, loves, and shares to feel good about myself.

My family is getting ready to move from Austin, Texas to Nashville, Tennessee. Why? Two reasons: one, because we can, and two, because we want to. In fact, by the time you read this, we'll have given away all but our most personal of belongings and hit the road in a modern-day convoy.

It took me a lot of years to get to this point. I feel comfortable in my skin and make choices based on what I want to do and only what I want to do. I have stopped caring what others think, say, or do about me (because they probably don't anyway). And I have stopped caring about what others think, say, or do in relation to whether I should think, say, or do those same things—unless they are highly interesting to me.

Why? Because, as I mentioned earlier, trying to live your life by someone else's rules and on their terms is exhausting and uninteresting.

I've made the choices that allow me to do what I want when I want—and you can, too.

I let go of what didn't serve me, and it landed me where I am today. You can do the same—I can almost guarantee it!

I know my life is easier and happier than most of the people I come in contact with. I can tell when someone is anxious, frustrated, depressed, and sad (or angry) because life hasn't turned out or isn't going the way they desire. Can't you?

3

HOW I DISCOVERED THE POWER OF AUTHENTICITY

I've discovered the power of authenticity on two memorable occasions in my life, which led to two personal Aha! Moments.

AHA! MOMENT NUMBER ONE

The first occurred during a particularly difficult time in my life. I let down my guard for the first time by accident. I found myself meeting with someone on a day when I would have liked to have stayed home, in a warm bed with the covers over my head.

I'm sure you can relate: a significant emotional event happens right before a meeting or event, and suddenly you're a hot mess. But, as they say, the show must go on, and at that moment, the show is you.

So, off I went, against my will and better judgment—when inside I was a bundle of *I could cry any minute*. And, also against my will, when the person I was with asked how I was doing, I couldn't hold it in. Tears leaked from my eyes and I was forced to admit *I was not okay.* As I shared with her what was going on in my life, I could tell she wasn't judging me (as I was sure she would). To my amazement, delight, and relief, she embraced me.

First, she said, *I'm glad you're human.* Next, she listened and validated my pain and suffering and made it okay to "have a moment." It was the beginning of what has become one of the most cherished friendships of my life. As a result of being authentic, we became very close friends and remain so to this day, almost twenty-five years later.

My first instinct—and I think this conditioning runs deep in our culture—was (and is) to present my best self, to pretend everything was A-Okay and keep myself and my problems to myself.

But on that particular day, I felt broken. Heartbroken. Hopeless. Sad. And I couldn't hold it together for one more second. Being authentic helped me to receive what I ultimately wanted anyway: love and acceptance, along with an incredible friend.

AHA! MOMENT NUMBER TWO

The second time was the beginning of my relationship with my husband, Byron. When we met I was a single mom and had been living in Las Vegas for a few years—not exactly a favorable combination for dating.

At the end of our first date he went in for the kiss, and I turned my head at the last second. I had decided, before our date, that no matter how much I liked him, there would be no kissing (or anything else for that matter). I may or may not have kissed on a previous first date, and here I was, still single. *Time to try something new, Honorée.*

Months go by, and we're still dating. Byron says to me, "So, what was up with the 'no kissing' on our first date?" And, I said, "I may or may not have kissed on a first date before. Still single and trying something new."

To which he replied, very wisely, "You can't do the wrong thing with the right person. And, you can't do the right thing with the wrong person."

And at that moment, a lot of life started to make sense to me. What I had known instinctively for years finally had words attached.

Being your authentic self is the way to be, and here's why: if someone is predisposed to like you, they're going to like you, pretty much regardless of what you do. And, if someone is predisposed *not* to like you, they're not going to like you (again, it won't matter what you do or don't do). There's pretty much nothing you can do to change someone's decision and opinion about you.

Said another way, from your perspective: if you don't like someone, they can't do anything right. If you like someone, they can't do anything wrong.

Trying *so fucking hard* to make people like you doesn't work. Being your authentic self allows the right people to become attracted to you, and the rest to choose out and go on their way.

I don't know about you, but I would prefer to have people around me who like me and enjoy my company (and give me a pass when I do or say something stupid). Anyone who isn't thrilled with me is free to be blessed and on their way. No harm, no foul, no judgment.

If someone meets me and doesn't like me, I'm cool with that. I don't like everyone either, especially people who aren't authentic. Can you relate?

I have too much to do, and *you have too much to do*, to give what someone thinks of you more than a passing thought. I hardly have enough time to make all of the people I cherish feel my affection and appreciation. I prefer to conserve my energy for loving on my family and friends, empowering my clients and audiences, and writing books.

You can choose to focus solely on the relationships that are best for you, and let the rest go. Living authentically means doing just that, and the benefits are too good to pass up.

JUST A FEW BENEFITS OF AUTHENTICITY

I'm going to cover the different facets of how you can stop trying so fucking hard and live more authentically in this book. But here's a sneak peek to get you started:

When you stop working to be someone or something you're not, you'll be astounded with the results. Being your authentic self allows you to be happier and have more fun. Saying *no* when you mean *no* may be hard at first, but you'll quickly love how happy you become.

What happens when you are happy? Only you know for sure, though I bet I can guess. You'll find yourself surrounded by happy people, doing happy people things, in happy people places.

Think about this: You can do so many amazing things with the energy you save by being authentic. You unleash your inner creativity when you don your #ZeroFucks T-shirt and crack open a super-sized can of authenticity.

You'll probably feel like doing things you know you should be doing, like spending time on hobbies and interests, hanging out with your friends, or even going to the gym.

Your authentic self is just sitting there, waiting to come out. Isn't it time to give her a chance?

I thought so, but first, let's visit "Reality.com" and identify where you are on the continuum of *trying too fucking hard.*

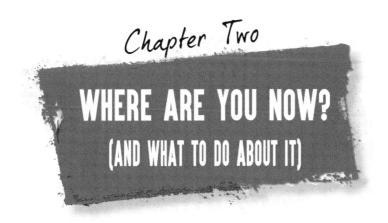

Chapter Two

WHERE ARE YOU NOW?
(AND WHAT TO DO ABOUT IT)

The individual has always had to struggle to keep from being overwhelmed by the tribe. If you try it, you will be lonely often, and sometimes frightened. But no price is too high to pay for the privilege of owning yourself.

–FRIEDRICH NIETZSCHE

SINCE YOU WERE EXPOSED TO OTHER PEOPLE YOUR AGE, probably in your first year of life, you've been conditioned to act, dress, learn, and be a certain way. The world-at-large implicitly and explicitly tells and shows us how to behave if we want to be accepted by others.

Depending upon where you grew up, you may have been expected to attend a certain school, do a particular type of work, marry your soulmate, have an exact number of children (two: one boy and one girl, or an heir and a spare), attend a specific church, support a particular political party, and even donate to the appropriate charitable causes.

There is nothing wrong with going the conventional path if it resonates with your soul. Going to the university your great-grandfather (and all of your other relatives) attended is great if you feel called to do so. You may, like many couples, meet your forever love in the third grade, get married right after graduation (high school or college), and die holding hands after sixty years of marriage. Being an accountant, lawyer, doctor, or banker might indeed melt your butter.

And if it does, if you wake up before your alarm and jump out of bed so fucking excited about another day of doing whatever you're doing, then why the hell are you reading this book?

Seriously, you are on the right path my friend, and your only homework is to keep doing it.

But if you're like *most people*, you're doing what you are supposed to be doing rather than what you want to be doing.

And that is a prime of example of *trying too fucking hard*.

HOW DO YOU KNOW FOR SURE IF YOU'RE TRYING TOO FUCKING HARD?

Said simply, you're trying too fucking hard if you're unhappy. Being unhappy is an action signal: a sign you need to pay attention and do something different(ly). Unhappiness is your own personal cocktail made up of nervousness, fatigue, panic, worry, hopelessness, addiction, comparing yourself to others, doing more than you want to, trying to force things to happen—and any number of other woes.

We live in a world that celebrates what we're *doing*, and not so much who we are *being*. People continually ask us what we're going to do next.

Upon graduation from high school, everyone wants to know where we're going to college. After college, we need to simultaneously climb the corporate ladder (or achieve something equally as important) while finding our soulmate, getting married, buying our first home, and having kids. As quickly and successfully as possible.

With all of these societal pressures and expectations, it is no wonder prescriptions for medication to treat anxiety and depression are at an all-time high. Suicide statistics are frightening. Almost everyone is addicted to something or knows someone addicted to something— and I'm not talking about good addictions. You know what I'm talking about: sex, drugs, alcohol, nicotine, porn, gaming, or some other activity designed to distract the doer from the true unhappiness they feel.

Unless you're on *the path* considered acceptable—dare I say, admirable—you probably won't get the support and encouragement you crave. And even if you are on an acceptable path, if you don't meet the bar set by those around you, you might feel judged rather than accepted.

In fact, you *will* be judged—mostly because those who are also not on the right path and feeling bad about it go out of their way to (a) keep their addictions secret while (b) loudly judging you for your lack of progress.

If you're the least bit different, it won't take long for someone in your family, neighborhood, community, or even church to give you a long stare and say, "Oh," when you share.

Perhaps you've drunk the Kool-Aid and are on the people mover, doing the best you can. If you've been succeeding and you're happy, great for you! Congratulations again, you're a unicorn and don't need this book. Give it to the guy in the next office—I can almost guarantee he's unhappy because truly happy people are few and far between. (If indeed you're the happy one, then odds are, most of the people around you probably aren't.)

You might be doing your best, but success hasn't come as quickly as you expected. You might feel "less than" or "not good enough" (hint: you *are* good enough) because you bought into the Ultimate Behavior Bill of Goods and you've followed the included instructions step-by-step, to the letter. So why aren't you on top of the world, feeling blissed out every single day?

Why? Yup, you guessed it. Because you're trying too fucking hard.

You're making great time, but your ladder is leaning up against the wrong wall. You're doing what you think you should be doing instead of doing what your heart wants to do.

As a business and executive coach, I couldn't tell you today the number of times I've worked with a "recovering attorney." Folks who went to law school because that's what was expected of them (plus they thought that would mean they would always have a job), later discovered they *hate being a lawyer*.

I'm not picking on lawyers, by the way. Insert "military officer," "therapist," "real estate agent," or even "full-time mom" for lawyer. The profession doesn't matter—what does matter is the fact that most people start their adult lives doing what they think they're supposed to do, rather than what they want to do. They haven't exercised their option to think for themselves and figure out what they truly want out of life. Then a decade or two later, they find themselves wondering "what the hell happened" and "is this all there is?"

The fact the primary question asked when making a new acquaintance is "What do you do?" (and automatically means profession and not hobbies or other interests) is, in my opinion, part of the problem.

We're categorized and characterized by our professions (and net worth), almost before and instead of everything else.

I'M GONNA BE HAPPY ... SOMEDAY

Not long ago, my husband and I got our daughter a car as her high school graduation present. When it came time to sign *all of the documents* (why are there so many documents?!), the delightful gentleman who helped us shared he had been a police officer for almost twenty-five years, and in the car business for almost fifteen more. He was working "just a couple more years," so he could have enough to send his youngest (who is just two years old) to college. *Then he would retire and be happy.*

One of my strategic book coaching clients shared he was bound by a pair of golden handcuffs: he makes "great money" in his day job, but truly desires to do something more creative, get his book written, and focus on his second career. But with multiple mortgages, a family to feed, and a lifestyle that requires constant funding, he was stressed and overwhelmed.

Sadly, these are just two examples from this month. I didn't have to work hard to think of people who were biding their time, hoping they would be happy "someday."

Both of these folks are great people. But they are trying too fucking hard. I have a feeling you might be, too.

ARE YOU TRYING TOO FUCKING HARD?

I don't have to talk to you one-on-one to know if you picked up this book, the answer is most likely *yes*. You're at the very least a little frustrated, and at most, hopeless and weary. You're wondering if there is another way, a different path you can take.

You might be trying too fucking hard if:

- You have to take a vacation a few times a year because you need a break from your day-to-day or you'll crack.

- You're taking medication because the stress and/or anxiety of your everyday life is too much.

- You're addicted to activities or substances you wouldn't want the world to know about.

- You eat or drink too much or not enough, or eat or drink as a coping mechanism or to numb your pain.

- You're always comparing yourself to others (in a negative way).

- You're engaging in attention-seeking behavior (ASB), such as posting, *I need a hug* on social media (as just one example).

- Your life is full of never-ending drama.

- You have an expensive lifestyle for the sake of being "that guy."

- You're trying to see and be seen by "all the right people."

- You're sourcing your decisions from the public-at-large.

- You're doing what you think you should do, rather than what you want to do.

As you can see, there are many things you might be doing that don't make you feel good, at best aren't constructive, and at worst are destructive—and they are all signs you're trying too fucking hard.

Lest you think I'm judging you for any of the above, I am not. I have love and compassion for you and know you're doing the best you can. When you know better, if to, you can do better. It is possible to unhook from behaviors you know don't serve you at the highest level, stop living in coping mode, and start embracing a happier, lower-stress life. But only if you want to, okay? Okay.

YOU'VE GOT OPTIONS!

I'm out here on the skinny branches, wearing my #ZeroFucks T-shirt, watching people twist themselves into a pretzel, and wishing they—you—knew there is an easier *and better* way.

Is it possible you could lay down your mantle, answer some thoughtful questions, and start living an easier and happier life? I think so. In fact, I know so. The answer, dear reader, is a resounding yes.

For every one of the actions mentioned above, you have another option.

- You can take vacations because you want uninterrupted quality time with your significant other, spouse, kids, extended family, girlfriends, or guy friends. Because that's fun (rather than as a distraction or coping mechanism)!

- You can engage in activities that counteract even the most significant stressors (like completing a project, moving to your dream home or a new city, or getting a promotion), such as journaling, visualization, meditation, or exercise.

- You can engage in a recovery program or even stop doing activities you know don't serve you and replace them with ones that do. You can take up fly-fishing or learn a new language or become a yoga teacher.

- You can make peace with food, eating to live rather than living to eat.

- You can have only those things and situations in your life you truly love and enjoy, and nothing extra or unnecessary.

- You can admire others for what they accomplish and use them as inspiration rather than comparison.

- You can surround yourself with amazing and supportive people who will fill your love cup, rather than seeking approval, validation, or endorsements from virtual strangers.

- You can have the right friends for you, rather than the right friends as determined by others.

- You can do what you want to do, every day for the rest of your life, starting today. You can, I promise.

These are just a few of the great things you can add to your life when you stop trying so fucking hard. When you're ready, turn the page, and I'll begin to show you how. First, let's do a reality check.

Chapter Three

REALITY CHECK

Comparison is the death of joy.

−MARK TWAIN

I KNOW YOU WANT TO KNOW WHAT THE "OTHER WAY" is (the one I just alluded to in the previous chapter). Before I share that with you, I think it's important we take a quick detour to "Reality.com." Of course, I'm cheeky, and my intention isn't to be disrespectful. You might not be picking up on my sarcasm, but make no mistake, it's there.

It is important to recognize, that in addition to my recommendation to utilize the advice of someone who is farther down the path you are on (or want to be on), that you are comparing apples to apples and oranges to oranges.

You might be thinking, *Good grief, Honorée, what on earth are you talking about?*

I mentioned it briefly in the previous chapter. I'm talking about comparison-itis. The act of comparing yourself to others, who just might not be as successful as they claim, or successful at all, or even the least bit qualified to be doling out advice.

If you're like most people, you compare yourself to others to gauge your progress. It's only natural to look at someone in your profession and compare number of years or sales, amount of money made, saved or invested, where you live, or even the cars you're driving.

The truth is, you might just be comparing yourself to something that is a complete and total fabrication.

Allow me to explain.

Appropriately timed, one of my colleagues posted on Facebook this morning: *Stop asking people for directions who have never been where you're trying to go.*

To which I added: *This includes taking business advice from people who don't own successful businesses, authors who have published less than a dozen or more books (and haven't sold hundreds of thousands of copies) or network marketers who haven't built a large downline.*

Doing something for a year, or a couple of times (or ONCE) does not an expert make. Seriously. Qualify your expert before you buy their program, course, or pay them for consulting or coaching.

The problem with comparing yourself to others, as I see it, is two-fold.

First, there's a group of "cool kids" who have seemingly achieved a level of success (many times unverified) and who proclaim they are the expert. As soon as they've reached the summit, they slap together a product to sell. Courses, weekend intensives, exclusive consulting—all available "for another 12 hours only!" for the low-low-low price of, well, don't buy it, folks!

In a fun twist of fate, these guys (and gals) seem to find each other (usually during high-priced, exclusive masterminds), co-sign each other's bullshit, and then band together and promote each other's stuff.

If that's not enough, you then enter the picture for the other half of this scenario.

Second, those who want to achieve success in their desired area follow these folks, see their glamorous and seemingly problem-free lives on social media, and compare themselves to an ideal that is, in fact, **fake news**.

I mean, God bless Facebook for allowing us to all keep up with each other. It is seriously cool that I was able to connect with my long-lost best friend from tenth grade after (ahem) thirty years. But seriously, folks, don't you realize most people (other than those with ASB who post their woes online to garner sympathy) don't put their true reality on display for all to see?

Here's the *real* problem: most of the cool kids aren't (in most cases) cool at all. Some of them aren't successful either, even though they appear to be. Perhaps they are successful in one area: they've made some money. Or, they've built and sold a business. They figured out one aspect of life or business, and then go on to create an entire platform touting their great success, even though they've not figured it out entirely. *Sometimes,* they aren't successful at all. They just pretend to be. And, they are human, just as you are, which means they experience the same doubts and challenges you do.

It's important to note it is easier to sell a program on how to be successful than it is to actually *be* successful. Some convince enough other people they've got a formula for success, then sell said formula (which is more sizzle than steak), and *that's* how they make their money. More people than you might realize are doing this. Keep that in mind when you want to give someone your money.

The truth is, and here's what's essential as it relates to you, my dear reader: the vast majority of these guys aren't happy or fulfilled. They struggle with internal doubt, anxiety, being discouraged, indecision, comparison-itis, addiction, even depression … sound familiar? I know, because I've had the distinct displeasure of interacting intimately with a number of them on multiple occasions. Lucky me.

If you knew just a fraction of the "behind the scenes" truth, you would be floored, as I was. Shocked. Appalled. I used to be, too. Now I think it's sad.

Publicly these folks are *all that*, and behind the scenes, trust me on this: they are a hot mess.

So, you can probably see how comparing yourself, your actual reality, to their front-facing "life is a bowl of cherries" faux reality can do more damage than good.

To you.

And here you are, comparing yourself to them, and probably beating yourself up because you're not as successful as they are. You can see how comparing yourself to others is not the best path to achieving a life of happiness or success, correct? (Nod and smile, please.)

My purpose, honestly, for this chapter is not to throw anyone under the bus. As I'm sure you have figured out, I'm wearing my #ZeroFucks T-shirt (all the time), so if on the off-chance one of them reads this book, I don't care. We know the truth; I think it is high time you do, too!

Now, *of course*, some actual super-cool kids are remarkable. Happy. Prosperous. Successful. Nice. Living in integrity and giving back to boot.

But at the end of the day, comparing yourself to them won't help either. I suggest you take their success as a sign you can do the same thing. Use their real accomplishments as a target, a goal, your desired outcome. Reverse-engineer their success into a solid plan you can enact and get busy making it happen. Compare your results to their results, as opposed to comparing yourself to them (unless you're crushing them, then that's okay). *Smile.

Please keep two important things in mind:

First and foremost, genuinely successful people rarely have time to post about how great their life is on social media. They don't need to do monthly income reports. Or to post pictures of themselves with anyone else (except their real friends and their family). They may post a rare picture here and there, and if they have a giving heart, a meme or quote of encouragement sprinkled in for good measure. You don't—and won't—see a lot of "look at me! moments" from professionals who are flourishing in their personal lives and careers. They are too busy making shit happen and getting things done.

> *I don't have a single client that owns a private jet that has EVER taken a selfie on it!*
>
> —STEVE SIMS, Founder, Bluefish

Success—real, lasting, perennial success—takes time. You cannot, simply said, "write and publish a book in thirty days." And yes, Virginia, you do need an editor. You won't be able to put on an extra fifty pounds of muscle, while shedding one hundred pounds of fat, between now and Labor Day if today is April 15th.

Multiple streams of leveraged income do not happen overnight. The 10,000-hour rule is a real thing, and it is in full force and effect. You don't get 10,000 hours of experience, training, certifications, and the grey hair that accompanies them in an actual 10,000 hours (more than 416 days). Even if you spend eight solid hours a day trying to master something, you'd better buckle up, wear comfortable shoes and take snacks—because that journey takes almost three and a half years. And that is based on a solid eight hours a day, seven days a week, twelve months a year—and does not include weekends, vacations, and holidays.

The person who encourages others to "get rich quick" or take a shortcut might fatten their bank account, increase their followers, and boost their egos. But they are not speaking the truth, at least not any truth that's going to help you.

I want you to be successful. Not for an hour (being a bestseller in your obscure category on Amazon does not make you a bestselling author), not for a week, a month, or even a year.

I truly want you to be successful, starting today, from now until you take your last breath (which is hopefully many decades from now). Happy at a soul level, successful in the way you define success, connected to others in meaningful relationships. These are the reasons I wrote this book, *for you*.

Because I want you to stop trying so fucking hard and relax into a life you love. Along the way, you can eliminate what many think are just the ordinary, expected stresses of life. In truth, they are self-inflicted and eliminate-able circumstances.

- Imagine having a career you love, something that mostly doesn't feel like work.

- Imagine having a relationship that lasts, where both parties think they've won the lottery.

- Imagine friendships based on mutual love, respect, and support.

- Imagine loving where you live, with great neighbors.

- Imagine having strong faith (in whatever peels your banana) to help get you through when times get tough.

Life will throw you curveballs. People will disappoint you. When you stop trying *so fucking hard* and put in place a life you truly love, you'll handle those obstacles with the same ease you ride over speed bumps at the mall.

You can enjoy waking up every day with a sense of purpose, feeling loved, content, and fulfilled.

Let's get you started, today.

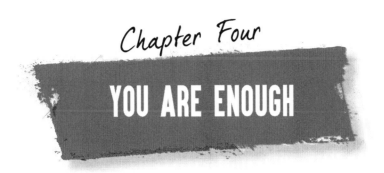

Chapter Four

YOU ARE ENOUGH

We buy things we don't need with money we don't have to impress people we don't like.

–DAVE RAMSEY, Author, *The Total Money Makeover: A Proven Plan for Financial Fitness*

THE FIRST STEP TO LIVING A LIFE YOU TRULY LOVE: *Stop trying so fucking hard.*

You've now heard me tell you this, several times. What *exactly* am I talking about?

This: You're trying to impress those around you— some of them you don't even know.

I observe people every day full of anxiety, comparing themselves to others, worried about what those others might be thinking about them, and trying to be something they're not.

And *you* …

You buy things you don't need with money you don't have to impress people you don't like *or even know*. You go places you don't want to go and do things you don't want to do. And for what?

So, you can post a pic on Instagram, showing how great (perfect!) everything in your life is?

What could you do?

Stop.

And listen to me now: *The only way to have a successful and happy life is to be your authentic self.* All. The. Time.

My co-author and friend Hal Elrod says, *Give up being perfect for being authentic.* And I couldn't agree more.

But while you're stuffing your authentic self way down deep, denying your true desires, and making everyone else happy (as if you could do that), you are missing out on the true joy and juice of life. You're burning your candle at both ends, running yourself ragged, over-doing, straining and striving to get there (wherever there is), all while looking to others for approval. Your significant other. Your family. Friends. Kids. Neighbors. Boss. Coworkers. People you barely know. It goes on and on!

And one-on-one, direct face-to-face approval isn't the only kind sought these days. Today, it's the likes, loves, and shares. The hearts. The comments and engagements. The sales, downloads, and rankings checked continuously. Refreshing screens over and over to see "what's new," what people are doing, and who to compare ourselves to in a way that doesn't serve us.

It seems as though the internal validation systems of people everywhere have been turned off in favor of gathering the external validation of family, friends, colleagues, and worse, Facebook friends or Twitter and Instagram followers.

It is easy to look at the lives of others, particularly those who write books, stand on stages, appear on television and in movies, and in other places of authority—and *want to be them.* Or, allow them to give us our opinions.

Anyone's life (save those with ASB, who post their woes online to garner sympathy) looks great from the outside. Instagram photos with the perfect filter show smiling faces, perfect abs, a delightful and fun life, wonderful in every way. Except …

What they don't show are the private struggles that almost (*almost*) everyone is dealing with—the bounced checks, cheating spouses, drug-addicted children, and back-stabbing business partners. Nope, not going to show that! But if they did, wouldn't you be able to relate more to them? Maybe so, maybe not.

Isn't there a better way? I say, *Yes.*

Yes, there is a more simple, effective, and joyful way to live. Here is a glimpse into what your excellent life can look like:

- You can adopt a clean, happy mental attitude, one that allows you to feel amazing, think clearly, and see things as they indeed are. *You can feel pretty great, almost all day, practically every day.*

- You can give equal weight to positive and so-called negative feedback from others. *You don't have to find yourself on cloud nine when you receive a compliment or face down in a pool of snot and tears when someone is rude, disrespectful, or abusive.*

- You can have only the people, things, and experiences (and more!) that bring you joy, make you smile and encourage you to be your best self. *You can have in your life only what and who makes you truly happy, no exceptions.*

- You can say yes or no as you see fit. *No is a complete sentence and requires no explanation. Your yeses must come out of your mouth with a feeling of excitement and enthusiasm.*

And those are just for starters.

You are a grown-ass adult. You can eat pizza for breakfast, down a liquid lunch, and suck down a dozen donuts for dinner. No one is monitoring this (and if there is, *why?*).

You can say *yes* or *no* depending upon what you truly want, and (newsflash!) those who truly love you will support you every step of the way.

Here's how I see it: as far as we know for sure, we only get one ride, one at-bat, one whirl on this rock. I hardly think we are supposed to be the least bit miserable.

To that end, I'm pretty sure we shouldn't spend a ton of time questioning ourselves, living in a pool of self-doubt, wondering if we're enough (and convinced we're not).

We should be enjoying ourselves, living life to the fullest, setting and crushing goals, laughing our asses off pretty much all the time.

Now for those of you who *do* eat pizza for breakfast, down a liquid lunch, and eat a dozen donuts for dinner, you may want to take a peek at whether or not that's what's best for your long-term health. There might be an opportunity for you to evaluate if food (or drugs, alcohol, sex, or Netflix) are an escape or coping mechanism. There are tons of books to help you figure that out, and this isn't that book.

This book is the book I hope will help you relax, release, relate, rejuvenate. Breathe better, break into bigger smiles, even indulge in a boogie or two. Spontaneous dance parties are fun, and if you haven't had one lately, how about now?

Note to yourself—if you have to force something, it probably isn't the right something.

What do I mean? Well, let me ask some questions:

- Are you in a relationship *you know isn't right (anymore)*, yet you are determined to make it work? Because you gave your word (perhaps in front of God and everybody) and that meant something to you?

- Do you have a boss, co-worker, or client who seems intent on making your life miserable, but you don't give your two weeks' notice, express your discomfort, or even stand up for yourself, *or* straight-up tell them to fuck off? Instead, you suffer in silence, telling your spouse, best friends, your mom, or even pay your therapist, for hours on end?

- Are you tolerating people or situations because you feel trapped, obligated, or even compelled to do so? You justify by saying, *It's not THAT bad.*

If none of these scenarios are present-time accurate, I'm sure at least one rings a bell. For me, too.

I've said the words *Suck it up, Buttercup* to myself on more than a few occasions. Sadly, we've all found ourselves biding our time and biting our tongues. More often than we'd like. More often than we should.

I'm not here to tell you to, or how to, engage with anyone and everyone within the sound of your voice. The point isn't to put anyone else in their place.

The point is to help you find your place!

When you stop trying so fucking hard, you'll do that all on your own naturally. Authentically.

YOU ARE GOOD. ALL GOOD.

The primary purpose of this book is to help you recognize, realize, and reap the rewards that come from embracing the fact that you are fabulous! You deserve the best right now, just the way you are (even as you seek to improve yourself).

You don't need *anyone else ever* to tell you this. You could know it and own it. But you've read this far, so I imagine you probably don't (yet).

With every person we come in contact with giving us "constructive criticism"—from the time we can walk to the commercials we see on television telling us we need buns of steel, to convert our currency, and grow our wealth—it is no wonder we constantly try to fit in while doubting ourselves every step of the way.

Allow me to repeat it: *you are enough*.

Just as you are now. At your current weight. Net worth. Marital status. Number of friends. Size of your family. Career. All of it. Enough.

And ... you're reading this book which tells me you want more. Fair enough. (Me, too.)

I've finally been able, after decades of self-development, to be grateful for where and who I am, even as I strive for more.

Yes, I want a flatter stomach, tighter buns, another comma in my net worth, and more sleep. And if I never accomplish another thing, I'm pretty cool with me as I am right now.

I'm not perfect and don't claim to be. What you see is what you get. I'm the same person privately as I am publicly. I swear (*obviously*), I get cranky, and I regret what I say sometimes. But I'm okay with me, and I want you to be okay with you.

You **could** decide you're okay and be done. If you're able to do that, you're done. Four chapters and you're all set. But if you need more, keep reading.

WHY ARE YOU ENOUGH?

If I'd written this book even ten years ago, I wouldn't have thought to answer the question *Why are you enough?* But I've had thousands of personal and coaching conversations since then, and I've yet to find a person who didn't need a few words of encouragement. Here you go:

One. You're alive. Whoever made you or however you got here (and I'm not debating the *how*), you did. That gives you the right to think you're pretty amazing. You don't have to do or say one thing ever to be deserving of every single incredible thing life has to offer.

Two. You are the only you! You have gifts and talents and abilities to give the world (and enjoy for yourself) that not one single other living person can share.

Three. Someone already loves you. Too late, you're loved and admired by people you know and people you don't.

Also: Because I said so. Ha! *smile And, I'm the author, which is short for authority and I know my stuff. Good? Good.

34

If you've been letting your lack of deservedness keep you from fulfilling a dream or achieving a goal, put an end to that shit today, okay? Let today be the last day you get in your own way, and fall prey to your self-destructive limiting beliefs. Allow yourself to start to dream again.

IT'S NOW ~~OR NEVER~~ ... AND FOREVER!

You're still reading, and I know you're ready to get some practical to go with the inspirational. (I mean, what is more unfulfilling than being all fired up and excited with nowhere to go?) I'm excited for you because I know how good life can be.

I wasn't joking about being the authority, and I thought it might be helpful if I touched on, briefly, why you might want not only to *read* my advice but also put it into practice.

If *Quitters Anonymous* were a thing, I'd be the founder. I haven't always kept my word, taken 100 percent responsibility, or thought I deserved the best. I've learned over and over again the pain and penalties of not sticking with a plan or following through until I reached a goal. You might reach a point like I did, where life wasn't working, and it was time for a permanent change.

Thankfully, I didn't give up. You haven't either, or you wouldn't be here. I want to share with you what I've learned, and for you to benefit from my learning.

Before I internalized these lessons, when the going got tough, this gal quit cold-turkey. I've started my fair share of projects and at the first sign of discomfort or inconvenience, pushed it off to a later date. I love fitness challenges—in fact, in any given month I'm doing at least one. But I started a half-dozen before I found out how to commit *100 percent*. I wasn't always a "no matter what" kind of gal. I could spin a weak excuse into a darn good reason—and convince you *like a boss*.

Lest you think that once you go "all in," life becomes a box of chocolates, think again. In fact, I was faced with the temptation to quit *this morning*.

Allow me to explain. Over this past weekend, with this manuscript due in less time than is comfortable in its current state, I agreed to write every morning *no matter what* with my gal pal April. For years I've written for an hour starting at 6 a.m., but in recent months I've been moving, nursing a sick relative, getting my daughter through graduation, and, well, procrastinating.

Not just a local move—several states away, to a place I've never lived. We're temporarily living with my husband's mom and her husband. His dad is in ICU for what could be months, and his wife, well, let's just say she's the inspiration for my first bestselling fiction thriller. I'm not even ready to talk about the stressful circumstances surrounding my daughter's graduation.

Any one of those is a reason to extend the due date on this manuscript, put my phone on *Do Not Disturb*, and take a long snooze. Right? Nope.

Enter: the writing buddy daily writing sprint challenge. Which started yesterday. April and I agreed to write every morning, beginning with a quick check in at 6:30 a.m. each day. Yesterday was great! In fact, I was up an extra hour early, took my mother-in-law to the airport, and was butt-in-seat fifteen minutes early.

Yesterday's production was top shelf, *Mesdames et Messieurs*. I mean, crushed it and my word count goal.

But today, well, today didn't start off as effortlessly.

I didn't wake up before my alarm. In fact, I woke up eighteen minutes late, wondering "what the hell," with just enough time to find a half cup of yesterday's coffee (blech), make a cup of tea in the microwave, and sit down to write. And here I am. Not to bore you with my tales of woe, but to let you in on the fact you will always experience challenges to your commitments. Usually and especially right at the beginning.

I could have begged off just one day, explained my situation, and April—being the great gal she is—would've understood entirely and given me a pass.

I can make fresh coffee in another 49 minutes. Right now, it's time to write. Not quitting and staying a person of my word is crucial to my success and happiness (and I'll explain why in the next few chapters).

Now, more than ever, it is important to me because I know at least one reader will write me and say this particular lesson changed their life. One of my issues with some persons of influence is they don't eat their own dog food. That is, they'll tell you to keep your word, but they won't do it themselves. That's reason *numero uno* for me to keep mine.

Doing what I say and saying what I do, I've learned, is crucial on the journey to success and happiness. I am psyched when I, sometimes against the odds, achieve something (no matter how small) when I could've delayed it or thrown in the towel.

If you've ever pushed through to victory, even once, you know what I mean! To step on the scale at your goal weight is amazing! To put a certain number of zeros behind your net worth feels incredible! Writing *The End* and turning your book in to your editor is a joy (and a relief). Cleaning out a closet, balancing your checkbook, going through that stack of papers, *finally*, and getting your desk in order can be epic.

Fast forward to today, after decades of consistent and constant, never-ending self-improvement, I am here. And glad to be so.

I can be happy alone or in a room full of people. I'm an introvert by definition (someone who recharges by being alone), yet I love people. My favorite thing to do is help another person. It doesn't matter if I hold the door open for them at the post office or change their lives forever, helping people makes me deliriously happy.

I've been thrilled to be married to my incredible husband for almost ten years. Though, as with any relationship, it hasn't come without challenges, disappointments, and stresses, but the blessings in this marriage far outweigh the challenges, and I'm grateful.

I have a terrific daughter. Having just graduated from high school, she's got a bright future, and I hope I'm a living example of what's possible for her.

I get to work with some of the kindest, most thoughtful, and brightest people on this planet.

Now, the concrete skills to turn wishes into reality are right around the corner. Ready? Let's do this!

Chapter Five

THERE IS ANOTHER WAY

There is no way to happiness. Happiness is the way.

-THICH NHAT NANH, Vietnamese Zen Buddhist Monk

I BET YOU'RE FEELING CAUTIOUSLY OPTIMISTIC, at least I hope so. That is how I would feel if I'd just read those first four chapters for the first time, and you might be getting impatient. Stay with me! *A lot* of people talk (and advertisers advertise) about how you can be thinner, richer, happier, and having more great sex than ever before—all in seven days or less! Why is this book different? How is what I say different?

I'm so glad you asked. *smile

I don't have a bigger agenda. I merely want to give you what you need to know to have the consistent feeling of someone who is at their goal weight, with a wad of cash in their pocket so big it's uncomfortable to sit down, a smile on their face so big you can see it from space, and as relaxed as one can be after a fantastic orgasm.

Don't worry. You didn't just start reading a naughty romance novel (but if that's your thing, check out my Author Notes, where I introduce you to one of the best "naughty romance" authors I know!).

I want you to *stop trying so fucking hard*.

TWO IDEAS TO GET YOU STARTED

There are two key ideas to get you started on your journey:

1. **Wear Your #ZeroFucks T-shirt**
2. **Attract Your Ass Off**

If you do nothing else I suggest in this book but adopt these two practices, you will be set for life. Combine them with the rest of my wisdom, and you're going to set the world—your world—on fire! And in a great way!

WEAR YOUR #ZEROFUCKS T-SHIRT

You're at least ten times smarter than the average bear, so I know you can *guess* what I mean. But I want you to be crystal clear on what it means to don this T-shirt. I want you to own it.

#ZeroFucks is an attitude you adopt. It is a position you take when you stop trying so hard.

It means:

- you know who you are, what you like and what you don't,

- *you give as much value to the good as the bad,*

- and you make no apologies for it.

If you're a woman over the age of 25, you've probably seen Julia Roberts' movie *Runaway Bride.* In the film, Julia plays Maggie Carpenter, a woman notorious for leaving men at the altar. Ultimately, she encounters the swoon-worthy Richard Gere and uncovers how she likes, among other things, her eggs.

She had spent her entire life liking what her multiple fiancés also liked, the way they liked it. Eventually, she decides to stop caring about what other people like and figure out what, as my friend Joe Carlisle says, *melts her butter.*

While you're searching for *Runaway Bride* on your streaming service, answer this question: do you know what you like? Do you know what you don't like? Are you able and willing to say *yes* only to who and what makes you happy, peels your banana, or melts *your* butter?

If you've been prone to liking (or hating) a particular political candidate, certain type of car, neighborhood, restaurant, or cocktail because of peer pressure, it might be time to reevaluate.

If you chose a profession because it was a family tradition, *and not because internal passion drove you,* it might be time to reevaluate.

A quick Google search for "#ZeroFucks T-shirts" led me to Redbubble.com (no affiliation with me) where I discovered lots of options, including the safer for work option of "Zero Fox Given."

Isn't it time for you to be happy? I hope you're nodding! Anything you do needs to be great for you. If you want to sell all of your worldly possessions and backpack around the world, do it. Ready to stop practicing law and open a yoga studio? Do it.

Order that #ZeroFucks T-shirt, put it on, and make yourself happy. Starting today.

ATTRACT YOUR ASS OFF

I have a hard-and-fast rule: if something is too hard, I stop. Whatever situation or relationship I've struggled to push forward in the past has almost always turned out to be a disaster. I've learned that trying too fucking hard usually leaves me in a bad way.

A more natural and better way is to become a person who attracts what they want. You can decide what you want, not know exactly how it's going to happen, and then get busy taking steps in the right direction. Then, you magnetize (yup, like a magnet) the thing, person, or situation you desire.

You are right if you think I'm combining the "out there, airy-fairy" Law of Attraction with some good old practical actions here.

Have you ever met someone who seemed to live a carefree life? Whatever they desired just came to them, even as they expressed their desire? I call it being in the flow, and it is a great place to be.

You might have wondered, "How much effort do I put into something, versus just sitting back and trusting a higher power?" I believe we co-create our lives with our higher power, (whether you refer to it as the universe or God or whatever). We have our part to play in getting what we want—but believe me when I say, our role is not forcing the outcome. Our role is one part intention, one part action, and one part trust.

You must do your part to magnetize your desire, which means first you need to show up! You can't just wish for something, and then go on about your life bitching and complaining. Thinking about your desires is not enough. You must intentionally get out there and set the wheels in motion, all while you're expanding both mentally and physically what you believe is possible for you.

Said another way: *As you pray, move your feet.*

To become a magnet for what you want, you will have to pass tests and learn lessons. You'll need to let go of any limiting beliefs around what you deserve and increase your self-esteem. To become attractive to your desired results will require identifying and eliminating any beliefs you have about yourself and the world in general that are preventing you from being your most magnetic, authentic self. And, you must adopt beliefs that serve you, encourage you, and allow you to take the steps you need to send out the signal to the universe-at-large that you are serious. You are serious about the thing you've said you wanted, and you're not (in a good, positive way) going to let anything or anyone stand in your way.

To that end, you will also have to let go of things and relationships that no longer serve you. During this move, I discovered I was holding on to a few things, books specifically, that I meant to read for years. I mean, if I hadn't made the time to read them by now, would I ever get around to reading them? Probably not. I wrote down the titles and donated them to Goodwill. Someone, somewhere, will get each of those books (and miscellaneous items and clothing) and it will be just the thing they need. That makes me happy. Bonus: I didn't have to move them, yet again, to a new home.

REJECTION IS PROTECTION

When we are rejected in love, life, friendships, or work, rejection can feel like *the worst*. In fact, we tend to internalize rejection and allow it to make us feel flawed, unworthy, or not good enough.

But I have a different take on rejection. I believe "rejection is protection." When we experience any rejection, it is a sign we need to take a different path, make another decision, or choose an alternate person.

I can look back on experiences that were, at the time, heartbreaking. They ultimately turned out to be blessings in disguise. In fact, had they turned out the way I wanted, my life would be completely different today (and not in a good way)!

The business I wanted to build sputtered and stalled, almost forcing me to discover a new route. Now I do something I love even more. My first marriage ended with a thud. Being single allowed me to work on myself and ultimately find and marry the love of my life.

I could go on and on, but now it's your turn. Can you identify past rejection that turned out to be the best protection ever?

Everything we experience in life directly supports our learning and growth, even if that rejection thoroughly sucks at the moment. The next time you're in the midst of experiencing rejection, instead of focusing on how awful you feel, ask yourself, "How is this rejection actually protection?" You might not even be able to see it until years later, but I promise you it's there.

ZERO F*CKS

And, as previously mentioned, you will have to start giving *zero fucks*. You simply have to stop caring about people and situations who don't deserve it.

Easier said than done, I know!

Attraction, otherwise known as the magnetism that comes from being authentic (and 100 percent responsible) will be instrumental in bringing what you want to you. Showing up for yourself, saying no to what is not serving you or what is making you feel small is critical to attracting.

...mate way to attract what you want is to become attractive to yourself.

KEEPING YOUR WORD

Honoring your word plays a considerable role in how people view you. It also ranks up there with determining how you see yourself. One of the fastest ways to simultaneously stop trying so fucking hard and upgrade your personal operating system (and attraction factor) is to become a person of your word.

In a world where being a person of our word matters, it is ironic so few people do. It is *so easy* to commit to anything and blow it off when the time comes to follow through or deliver. To be vague and ambiguous and leave people wondering. But for the most part, leave others wondering if they can count on you and trust you and you've set yourself up for failure.

When you're a person of your word, you don't have to try so hard to make others like you. They won't be able to help themselves because they will know you say what you mean and mean what you say.

Keeping your word is only one piece of the equation.

A person of their word:

- says only what they can and will do,

- does what they say they will do (or a little more),

- and, renegotiates when the going gets tough.

Let's take that one step at a time, shall we? Being a person of your word isn't complicated. Before you say something (i.e., make a promise), take a moment to consider if, when, and how you'll be able to deliver. If you're confident you're good to go, commit.

If, for some reason, you have any hesitancy, don't make a statement that commits you. Instead, say exactly and only what you can and will do. If the other party isn't happy with you or what you're able to do, you may be in for some negotiation (especially if that party is your boss).

Now you're on the hook—but if done correctly, you're all set. You said what you could do, and now you can do what you said. And, when you can, do a little more. Under promising allows you to overdeliver like a champ—and let me tell you, people love it when you surprise them (in a good way).

You might be wondering what you're supposed to do if circumstances change and you're unable to deliver on your promise. I've got you covered! Here's what you do: renegotiate your agreement.

BAD NEWS NEVER AGES WELL

The very moment you realize you are unable to deliver what you've promised, have another conversation. *I know I said I could do X, but then this happened, and now I'm only able to do Y. Does that work for you?* Sometimes it will—in fact, most of the time it will because almost no one ever renegotiates ahead of the curve. They fail to deliver and hope nobody notices or is upset.

Acknowledging you're unable to follow through is a cornerstone of a person of their word. Calling it out and ensuring it is okay with the other person is the honorable thing to do.

You can use this with major deadlines or when you're going to be ten minutes late to a meeting. By all means, don't make the other person chase you down! I'm highly frustrated when someone misses a deadline with me and doesn't even bother to acknowledge it. Don't compound a problem by failing to make your promise and leave it unacknowledged.

One final tip you may find comes in handy: asking the question, *How can I make it up to you?* When you don't keep your word, it might not be a big deal. Or it could be a huge deal! Nine times out of ten, when I ask *How can I make it up to you?* the response I hear is, *Don't be silly. It's fine. Do what you can.*

Owning the gap between the original promise and what you're able to do now is key to keeping trust and respect in the relationship.

When you're trying too fucking hard, you're promising a lot and delivering, well, not so much. Flip the script, and you will be respected and have respect for yourself.

BUILDING YOUR TRUST MUSCLE

Another component of attraction is building your trust muscles. You're human, and unless you have lived a sheltered life void of disappointment and hurt, you have experienced bouts of shame, depression, or low self-worth. As a result, it isn't always easy to trust yourself, the universe, God, other people, or anything or anyone.

In fact, we not only have our experiences to back us up, but we also have our teachings to keep us in line. We have been taught you have to work hard (as opposed to smart). We're taught if something isn't hard, it isn't worthwhile! We must suffer in relationships, to get that advanced degree, or push through to get the deal.

Whoa, just whoa!

Life should be easy. Relationships should be easy. Work should be easy. Full of laughter, aha! moments, and joy. You will, of course, have difficult times, encounter challenging situations, people, and events. That's life! But overall, we are meant to thoroughly enjoy ourselves, one another, and our trips around the sun.

Because I believe that, I believe we still must trust there is a bigger plan. And we must keep our trust muscles strong. We have to strengthen them over time, even as we experience disappointments and challenges.

What strengthens those muscles? As you attract or manifest small magical things and bigger miracles, your muscles go from small to big. Your muscles get stronger and stronger.

The first step is to really listen to your thoughts and words and hear what your inner voice is saying. What are you saying "I can't" to? How are you phrasing your desires? Always remember the universe hears the noun, not the modifier—so if you say, "I want to have no debt," the focus is still on debt and the universe hears "debt." When you change it to "I want financial freedom," the universe hears something completely different—and soon you'll notice you're closer to having financial freedom.

If thoughts become things, what thoughts are you manifesting?

The bigger the manifestations get, the stronger your muscles get, the more you trust. If you are someone who doesn't yet have a ton of trust or believe in manifesting and attracting, you'll need to open your mind first, and then begin by taking the first step. And then another. And then another.

Decide what you want. Make a plan. Open your mind to the possibility it could happen. Determine the best first step. Then, take that first step. The universe will respond by starting to gift you with signs and clues you're moving in the right direction.

You might notice, as I did, that when I'm on fire, fired up, or just feeling pretty good, more often than not, good things happened. The reverse is also true—anytime I'm wearing my cranky pants or slip into a tiny bit of complaining (no, really, it happens!), I will get a tiny warning I'm not on the right path. If I fail to correct my course, I'll get a swifter kick in the ass (the ones that hurt). I'm fairly pain-averse at this point; I try to heed tiny warnings, so I don't end up in traction.

I call these intentional actions "raising my vibration," which again, may sound pretty esoteric. So, here's the practical path: listen to fun music, watch a funny movie, break a sweat (on the elliptical or in bed with your paramour, doesn't matter). Do something that makes you feel good, and then do your best to keep those good feelings going.

Some people feel more comfortable with more acceptable terms, like raising their self-worth. Whatever works for you, do that. It is widely known in psychological circles you must raise your self-esteem in the exact ratio to what you want to bring into your life. In fact, this personal expansion is the catalyst that brings, or magnetizes, what you want. A big part of attraction is building your trust muscle, which requires raising your self-esteem and feelings of deservedness.

VISUALIZE IT!

While you're adjusting your attitude to eliminate all of your fucks and you're becoming a magnet for all you desire, I've got some pretty cool news: you can help speed things up by using the power of visualization.

Some people get stuck when trying to incorporate visualization. The truth is, you visualize all the time. Before you get out of bed, you imagine grabbing a shower, stopping at Starbucks on the way to your first meeting of the day, and the dozens of other actions you'll take that day. In fact, we visualize most everything we do before we do it (sometimes just moments ahead of time).

I'm going to suggest one of the faster ways to stop trying so fucking hard *and* get the results you desire is easy and free. Truly, you can transform your life by using the supercomputer that sits squarely between your two ears.

I first used visualization as a 9-year-old, training for my first marathon. My goal for an entire year was to finish the Athens Marathon. I would visualize starting the race, running fast and feeling strong, then finishing in the Ohio University football stadium. I would train along the course, finishing some of my training runs in that stadium, running along the bike path during the final miles of the race. Every time I finished a training run, I'd imagine I was finishing the full 26 miles, 385 yards. It is no surprise that when race day came, the finish was much like I had imagined it dozens of times.

Twenty-five years later, in 2004, I attended the PSI Basic Seminar, during which I was taught the "Screen of the Mind" technique. Maxwell Maltz taught a similar technique and called it the "Theater of the Mind" in his book, *Psycho-Cybernetics*, which I had read years earlier.

The phrase "Theater of the Mind" originally characterized the way classic American radio dramas invited the listener's imagination into a story. It's a phrase very familiar to traditional radio folks but not as well known by the public at large. In the years since radio dramas were a *thing* (and especially since the advent of

TV in the 1950s), the use of our imaginations has gone by the wayside, and with it, a lack of desired results!

So, what is it? The Theater of the Mind used only spoken words and sounds to paint a picture in the listener's mind, which they could then fill in the "gaps" with their imagination. It was, and is, a powerful creative device for conveying action (*the rumbling engine of a passing truck*), expressing emotion (*a booming voice*) or creating a sense of place (*crashing waves*).

What is impactful about tapping into the power of your own Theater of the Mind is that it gives the user—you—a vivid, believable experience. *First you experience your desired outcomes in your mind, then those mental experiences become your reality.*

Cool, right? So cool!

You can work with your vision and goals for your life mentally first, and spend time visualizing your positive outcome. (Bonus: it's completely free!)

Once I realized how powerful my subconscious mind is, and learned how to tap into its power effectively and efficiently, I was all in.

I re-named it my Mental Workshop, in which I have a *screen* in my *theater*. While I kept it pretty simple at first, over time my Workshop has evolved into a fun place for me to spend time creating my future. Today, it has a snack bar, a roundtable of advisors (a technique from Napoleon Hill's *Think & Grow Rich*), very comfortable chairs, and the latest technology. All created within my imagination! I use my Mental Workshop to solve problems and envision a successful outcome to challenges. It helps me to effectively envision positive results in my creative pursuits and visualize the perfect and easy attainment of all of my goals and objectives.

Before I have coaching calls, give speeches, or even have tough conversations, I spend some time in my Mental Workshop visualizing the ideal outcome. I highly suggest you do the same.

CREATING YOUR MENTAL WORKSHOP

You can create a Mental Workshop to produce results mentally first, with intention and purpose. Just as you would build your dream home with certain qualities and characteristics to suit your personality and desires, so can you create your Mental Workshop.

To create your Mental Workshop today (is there going to be a better time?), go to a quiet place where you won't be disturbed. If possible, do a five-minute silent meditation. There are several on YouTube. Next, follow these three steps:

Step One: Imagine you are entering your favorite room, with the most comfortable chair you've ever had the pleasure of sitting in. One armrest reveals a control panel for the giant movie theater-like screen on the wall in front of you. The other armrest has one button that summons a desk that appears when you think of it (or you need to research something), another for your male and female advisors (these are the two people you can ask to do tasks or provide insight and information).

Step Two: Add advisors to your roundtable. You could have Einstein help you invent something, Steve Jobs for inspiration or to develop new ideas, or even Dr. Oz to help you diagnose and heal a worrisome condition. You might have someone you admire in real life (IRL) but don't know them all that well. If you value their opinion or would pay for their advice, by all means, add them to your advisors. You will be amazed at the answers you get when you ask them questions!

Step Three: Spend time in your Mental Workshop every day practicing silence, gleaning advice from your advisors, solving problems, visualizing your goals as achieved, and even building out the space more as time goes by. Mine is now multiple stories, and I have rooms I go into for different projects or even conversations.

USING YOUR WORKSHOP

Next, use these five tips to master the use of the Mental Workshop technique.

Have a specific time and place that you use your Mental Workshop. The habit of daily use creates proficiency, and you'll enjoy it more the longer you do it. After a guided meditation, I spend about ten minutes in my Mental Workshop before I hop out of bed in the morning.

1) Imagine entering your Mental Workshop, getting comfortable, maybe pop some mental popcorn and grab some sparkling water with lemon (or some apple slices with some hot tea; I love a good cinnamon-spiced hot tea).

2) To get great results, visualize the end result exactly as you want it to happen. Don't worry about the *how*. Just as you see athletes visualize the perfect high jump or free throw before they make an attempt, you can do the same for any situation, goal, or outcome. The more clarity you have before you begin the visualization process, the faster you can visualize what it is you want. And, the quicker you will experience the result!

3) Imagine feeling what you will be doing, doing what you will be doing, and/or having what you want to have *as if you were already experiencing it right now*. What would it feel like to be driving in that new Bentley or holding hands with the perfect person in your new relationship (or celebrating twenty-five years of wedded bliss)? The more authentically you can feel, do, and have the experience in your mind, the more likely you are to manifest what you desire—and the faster it will show up, too!

4) You can use your Mental Workshop to help you produce results in all areas of your life. Use it to resolve resentment, to create positive outcomes that you desire, and to manifest opportunities.

The bottom line is to get in the habit of spending time in your Mental Workshop to create the life you desire. It is much easier to attract than to force results. It can become a very valuable tool. Remember, *it works when you work it!*

WHEN TO SAY YES! (OR NO!)

One more important facet in your "there must be another way to live" pursuit is knowing when to say *yes* and when to say *no*. Just as we've been pressured to conform how we are as human beings, we've also been pushed into doing or not doing, depending upon what's cool (or not) or in (or out).

All the girls are taking dance, so we must also. All the boys play football, so don your pads and helmet and get out there! It doesn't matter if you'd rather curl up with a good book or study the theory of relativity. The logical and practical choice of professions is the one in which you can make the most money or achieve the level of fame desired.

But are those activities what you want to do?

Everyone marries after dating a year or so, has kids, buys a house, nicer and nicer cars, vacations in Hawaii— et cetera and so on.

But do you want to get married? Have children? Own a home? Maybe so, maybe not.

You may have complied in varying degrees up until now, with some things working out better than others.

It should come as no surprise I'm going to ask you to carefully evaluate every relationship, activity, and situation you're currently involved in to determine if you should keep on keepin' on.

The other option, and dare I say the better way to go, is to notice how you truly feel and what you think as you're moving through your days. As you are going from conversation to conversation, and from place to place, notice how you feel. Are you excited or reticent? Positive or pensive?

I did what I thought I was supposed to do for far too long, and without boring you with my tale of woe, suffice it to say it didn't work out so well.

I've transformed how I consider engaging in something new or with someone new. For me, my answer is intuitive and so simple it almost seems cliché.

Whether I'm asked to collaborate on a project, take on a challenge, or even see a movie, I've learned to listen to my gut, and it never steers me wrong. I'm either a "Hell yes!" or "Hell no!"

Some answers take longer than others. If I'm unsure right away, I'll wait until my daily meditation and can hang out in my Mental Workshop so I'll be able to hear my internal, quiet voice.

When Hal Elrod asked me to talk about writing another book in the single mom series, my first thought was *I'm done with books for single moms—six is enough!* But my small voice said, *Have a conversation.*

A question from my daughter prompted a move to Austin from Las Vegas, and a brief conversation with my husband prompted our move to Nashville. Thankfully with freedom comes choice, so we could make both moves with ease.

Opportunities and requests—to say *yes* to a new relationship, take a new job, hang out with a new friend, or even go to a movie—happen every single day. It might be that up to this point you've been saying yes all the time (we'll address *that* in the next chapter) instead of only when you want to. If the idea gives you pause, offer a polite *no* and keep on going. On the other hand, if something makes your heart sing, give it a go!

As you begin to listen to your inner voice and doing only those things you want to do, you'll naturally be able to stop trying so hard and start living in the flow.

Now you know a few of my secrets for a happy life and are well-armed to do the same for yourself. In the next chapter, you'll learn everything you need to know about fear (and how to use it to your advantage). I'm ready when you are!

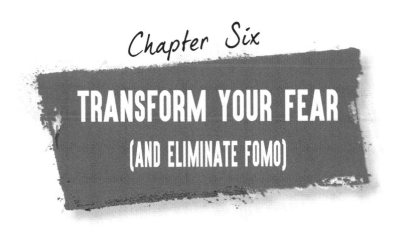

Chapter Six

TRANSFORM YOUR FEAR
(AND ELIMINATE FOMO)

*You gain strength, courage, and confidence by every
experience in which you really stop and look fear
in the face. You are able to say to yourself,
"I lived through this horror. I can take
the next thing that comes along."*

-ELEANOR ROOSEVELT

PEOPLE WHO ARE TRYING TOO FUCKING HARD, I'VE FOUND, spend a lot of time afraid. They are fearful of what *might* happen and spend time imagining the worst possible outcome.

In fact, if I had $10 for every time a friend or client has called me and started a story with, *I woke up this morning in a complete state of panic,* I could buy you a pony.

Fear, also known as *being afraid, in a panic*, or *feeling dread*, is a vital response to physical and emotional danger—if we didn't feel it, we couldn't protect ourselves from genuine threats. Often, we fear situations far from those we could classify as life-or-death. Mentally labeling a situation, event, or even a person as a threat, or deciding that pursuing a goal could be too big of a risk, puts us squarely in our own way, eliminating the many possibilities of success, connection, or joy.

Stress even has its roots in fear. As we worry about a situation, our worry increases our stress levels, as does our fear of what we think might be the outcome.

If you allow fear to run your life, you can find yourself in the darkness of your deepest anxieties. Fear can cause you to seek solace and distraction in the pursuit of money, food, and other nonproductive activities that won't in any way get you what you want.

Fear asks a lot of *What if...?* Questions:

- *What if it doesn't work out?*
- *What if I suck at this?*
- *What if I get rejected?*
- *What if this or that happens?*
- *What if I fail?*
- *What if I don't do this and miss out or am judged?*
- *What if I miss out?*

What if ... questions can be empowering, but not these! These questions, and any questions asked with a supposition, lead you to answering from a place of fear. In a state of fear, you can hardly be expected to have the presence of mind to answer *What if it doesn't work out?* with a strong and confident, *It always works out—for the good of all concerned!* It becomes difficult to answer *What if I'm judged for not doing that?* with a self-assured, *I don't want to do that, and I don't need to care what anyone else thinks about it!*

FEAR CAN BE YOUR FRIEND

Fear is innate and completely natural. It is a built-in response meant to protect us and keep us safe. It keeps us from getting too close to the edge of a cliff. It can be an internal driver that keeps us going when we're tempted to stop. Fear can help us to slow down when we're moving too fast or speed up when we're moving too slow. Using your fear can be a good thing.

Here's a fear of mine: *If I don't keep working I'll end up living in my car.* That fear, however ridiculous, gives me drive, and this internal drive keeps me moving forward.

You can make friends with your fear (and its close cousin, anxiety) and use both of them to your advantage. Fear can be useful when used as an internal motivator, or to see things from a different perspective. Actors use their fears to help them get into an authentic place for their on-screen and on-stage roles. You can use your feelings to get better at what you do. When you can integrate processing your issues into your work or any other constructive outlet, it will help you in ways you wouldn't expect.

In your creative pursuits, work, dealing with difficult people, and even in your search for a better financial or educational position, learning how to channel your fears can drive you to new levels of success. Your desires to win, be of service, or take care of yourself and your family can originate in your fear.

The truth is, you can keep those fears from running your life—or said another way, prevent you from *not* running your life! A terrific alternative is to put them into perspective, harness them, and use that energy to propel you forward. Transforming your fear into positive energy you can use to keep things in perspective and propel you forward is possible!

Let's unpack that a little, shall we?

HOW TO TRANSFORM YOUR FEAR: TOOLS AND STRATEGIES YOU CAN USE

A wise friend once told me, *When you're embarking on something new, if you're not scared you're not doing it right.*

What does that mean, "doing it right?" It means admitting you're afraid and recognizing that in a particular moment, you don't know where to begin, how to start, or even how to move. It could also mean if you aren't afraid, you aren't going for something big enough. Either way, being afraid isn't bad!

No matter what's got you stuck: a divorce, the illness or death of a loved one, or thinking about your kids growing up and leaving the nest, you would be well-served to do an exercise that has helped me many times.

First, ask yourself, *What, or who, do I need most to manage this situation, handle this crisis or, in some cases, survive?* You might need to find a quiet space to pencil out your options. You may want to sleep on a major decision. You may need to seek the counsel of your mom, best friend, clergy, or therapist (or all of the above). It might be time to put your phone on Do Not Disturb for a few hours or days to give yourself the space to think, meditate, nourish, or heal.

I *do not* do my best work or make my best decisions when I am tired, hungry, or at less than 100 percent physically. Part of my self-care regimen is to do my best to rest and eat on a schedule (and I am an expert napper). I've learned to give myself extra grace when I'm under the weather. It will serve you to figure yourself out and how to operate at your highest level.

When confronted with a tough situation, it's good to talk it through with someone, the *right* someone. It takes courage to show our true, vulnerable selves to others, and hopefully, you have at least one person you trust implicitly to give you quality feedback, information, and advice. If you feel like you don't have a friend in the world, then not only will you benefit from becoming attractive to yourself, you will also want to seek the services of a trained professional. A great therapist is a game-changer.

Once you've identified what or who you need, go on to the next step.

Second, determine what you need to do and what you need to not do. Whether you are sad, angry, frustrated, or feeling defeated, there is a list of things you might want to do, such as come up with several solutions, get organized, or break a sweat. You might want to *not* say something in anger, stalk your ex on social media, or eat those two whole pizzas all by yourself.

Third, keep this good news in the back of your mind as you process the situation: **This too shall pass.** And it will. You know that. You will encounter stops and false starts as you work through the emotional stages associated with your situation. You *will* figure it out. You *will* come out the other side a happier and calmer person. You *will* realize that you are a much stronger person than you thought you could be.

Remember any challenge is an opportunity for growth. You're participating in this great human drama called life, so if you're not in the middle of something now, you will be before you know it.

Even as you're coping with uncertainty and insecurity, you can use a few guaranteed tactics to kick out the demons of self-doubt and instill some certainty and calm:

REMEMBER YOU ARE IN CHARGE.

When you're tempted to say or do something at the height of intense emotion, ask yourself: *Is this me or my ego?* Our egos can be nasty little devils who, if left unchecked, will have their negative way with our thoughts. Ego is responsible for those 3 a.m. gremlins who wake you, jump up and down on your bed, and shout, *You can't do that! Who do you think you are?* Or *Go ahead, tell that bitch where to go!*

Feed your brain loving thoughts. After all, your subconscious mind believes everything you tell it! Sit up in bed and tell your ego, *Go away and leave me alone. I need to sleep. Also, waking me up at 3 a.m. isn't going to get you any favors!*

When I am short on patience, I have been known to say, *Not today, Satan!* So, feel free to use that whenever you'd like.

If even that doesn't help, change your energy! Do some yoga or go for a walk, listen to classical or other inspiring music, or put on an audiobook or podcast that always inspires you. I'll add my beautiful editor Alyssa's note here:

> *I use water to change my energy or my kids' energy. If they're in a funk and need to let the bad emotions drain away, I throw them in the shower, tub (especially with Epsom salts—salt being an emotional cleanser), or pool. I'm a fan of showers for me. I visualize the fear, sadness, yuckiness, whatever, going down the drain as the water washes over me. Works a treat for both me and the kids.*

KEEP YOUR JOURNAL HANDY.

Next to your bed is a great place, so you can grab it and start writing anytime you'd like. Through journaling, you'll either reveal a gem that helps you, or you'll get tired and fall asleep. Either way, you'll dump your fears onto the written page and out of your brain. My trainer posts journal prompts in our Facebook group every evening for us to use during our early morning journaling. Here are a few of my favorites:

- I'm committed to …
- What are the biggest lessons I've learned on my journey?
- What is this situation trying to teach me?
- What are my top three favorite accomplishments?
- If I weren't afraid to fail, I would …

Spending even five minutes answering the above questions can and often does reveal hidden gems. Another option is to read *The Artist's Way* by Julia Cameron and begin to practice the Morning Pages.

Journaling is a great way to figure things out as well as record life events. Be sure to lock it up if there are prying eyes—your journal is solely for you, so be sure to protect your privacy if that might be needed.

LAUGH OFTEN.

Keeping your sense of humor and laughing at least daily is sanity- (and life-) saving. I suggest saving some humorous reading material on your nightstand. This will come in handy at the end of a rough day. Reading something to make you spit out your tea because you're laughing so hard you're in tears is a great way to cap it off. At the very least, cue up some cat videos on YouTube.

I started appreciating humor's power and stress-relieving abilities when I read Reader's Digest in high school (also known as one of the most stressful times in my life). I discovered and immediately loved their feature, *Laughter Is the Best Medicine*. Don't think you need a tremendous amount of stress to benefit from laughing—although I know more than one person who has healed themselves from life-threatening diseases by watching non-stop comedy routines (try *Raw* by Eddie Murphy or some videos by comedian Sam Kinison).

LISTEN UP!

Music or inspirational tapes are two ways to feel better almost instantly. Load up your iTunes with "inspiration on demand," then insert your earbuds and turn up the volume. If you're interested in feeling better faster, combine listening with moving (see my next point, Move It!).

My favorite motivational speakers include:

- Tony Robbins
- Mel Robbins
- Dr. Maxwell Maltz
- Marie Forleo
- Jim Rohn
- Brené Brown
- Dennis Waitley
- Esther Hicks
- Mark Victor Hansen
- Zig Ziglar

I'll spare you my musical preferences and instead share a brief story. The day Michael Jackson died, I was driving to a meeting about ten minutes from my home. Like most everyone, his death was a shock. I grew up on MJ and thought his passing was untimely and a loss for the world. On my way to the meeting, the radio DJ came on, talked a little bit about Michael, and introduced a two-pack: the first song was "You Are Not Alone." This song, of course, brought me to tears. Within about two minutes, I had tears streaming down my face and was in need of a hug! Thankfully, the next song was "Beat It." Of course, the second song is upbeat, catchy, and thankfully, happy. It didn't take long for the tears to dry up and my mood to shift from sad to happy and grateful. I was able to pull myself together before I got to my meeting.

All because of music.

My point is simply this: you know what artists and songs light you up (and, of course, the ones that help you do the ugly cry). Do yourself and your mood a favor and identify the ones that make you dance in your seat, run a little faster, or inspire you. You can't go wrong with a *Rocky* soundtrack, and there are lots of pre-made running or dance mixes available. Hop on Spotify and put together the mix that helps you feel more "Beat It" and less "You Are Not Alone."

MOVE IT!

Taking a brisk walk or having a spontaneous dance party makes you feel better in a flash—especially if you've got some good stuff flowing in through your ears! For those of you with high-energy (or desiring more energy), roll into your workout gear and take an invigorating walk or go for a run. Or turn on your fancy new playlist and dance like it's 1987. Any of these are guaranteed to release endorphins, nature's way of feeling good. Not only are endorphins thought to block the sensation of pain, but they also work to lower stress levels and support the immune system. And you can release those suckers anytime you want—all you have to do is shake your money-maker. *Smile.

HAVE A GOOD CRY.

Crying is an excellent release, and you can cry those fears right the hell out. If you are generally not a crier, rent a tear-jerker of a film like *Beaches*. My husband says *Old Yeller* is guaranteed to shake loose even a tough guy's waterworks. A good cry will release toxins while simultaneously allowing you to put your fear in perspective. Do you remember your mom telling you to *Have a good cry!* Your mom is still smart, she knows. Listen to mom.

CALL BULLSHIT.

Fear is a big bully, so stand up to it and punch it in the nose. Like any bully when faced with a substantial challenge, it will back down. I mean, how right can your fear be? It can't be right all the time, and it probably isn't right this time, either. Be sure to question your fear like you'd question the person who wants to care for your small children or elderly parents in your absence. Keep in mind that when you start to raise your vibration, your nervous system *will* freak out and present you with oodles of fears. Going from your "normal" up to a new and higher vibration is as uncomfortable (or more) and unsettling to your subconscious mind as finding yourself in lack and limitation. You will need to stay vigilant! Recognize it when it happens and think of your fear emotions as coming from an overly-concerned Aunt. Look at her and tell her "I hear your concern. I know you're worried for me. But I've got this."

Say to yourself, or even out loud, if it would help, *Nope, I'm not listening. You can't get me down. I've got this!* Watch it shrink and run away quick like a bunny.

LET GO OF FOMO: FEAR OF MISSING OUT

I have zero *fear of missing out.* Why? For two reasons: first, I don't need to do anything or see anyone to be happy. Second, I believe I'm always in the right place at the right time.

If I stay home, that's where I'm supposed to be. If I'm out in the world, at that moment, that's where I'm supposed to be. If I'm supposed to see that Facebook post, Instagram photo, or *Breaking News!* story, than I will. Chances are, if I missed it the first time, I'll hear about it at just the right time.

FOMO seems to be plaguing folks right and left. The worst thing you'll miss out on isn't a party, late-night karaoke, or the chance to win. What would be truly tragic is if you missed out on a lifetime of being truly happy.

Don't believe the hype! The grass isn't always greener, and the folks out tying one on aren't necessarily having more fun. There's no need to second-guess your decision to RSVP "No, thank you" to an event when your heart isn't in it.

As we've previously discussed, when you spend some time in quiet contemplation, you'll be able to trust your intuition. That still, small voice is an excellent guide when deciding to go or stay.

If you've been using the mantra, "I don't have enough time to…" (insert cool goal here), chances are you've been spending your time engaging in some FOMO-based activity. I wouldn't be able to learn foreign languages, get regular pedicures with my daughter, or read a couple of books a week if I lost time on social media, answering every email the minute I received it or said "Yes!" to every invitation.

FOMO is an action signal something needs to change. Use that antsy feeling as a sign it's time to do something new: take a class, move to a new city, or take up yoga. Ask yourself these questions:

- What exactly am I afraid of missing?
- Why do I need to be busy constantly?
- What's on my wish-list of things to do, I haven't gotten around to doing because of FOMO?
- What need am I trying to fill?
- Am I happy spending time alone, just with myself?

Once you've answered those questions, take some time to sleep on the answers. Make a new master wish list of things you want to do in this lifetime. Then, spend some time clearing your calendar of tasks and to-do's. Chance are you'll find a significant amount of white space, and in that space, you can place the activities that will bring you maximum joy. The next time you find yourself with a spare hour, or day, you'll know just what to do with it!

There's one last piece to eliminating the majority of your fears: learning your lesson.

LEARN YOUR LESSON.

As luck would have it, your trepidations, middle-of-the-night panics, and free-floating anxieties can be some of life's best teachers, which may seem counterintuitive. But how you're feeling might be an action signal—a sign you should change your perception or your procedure. Your so-called negative emotions can help you do better, be better, especially if you listen, pay attention, and learn.

What is your fear trying to tell you? Listen carefully to learn whatever the lesson is (and not repeat it). Fear can be a critical component for change, giving you a chance to change the "hole" you feel to the "whole" of a new, re-invented, re-defined you.

It turns out my friend was right: if you don't have some fear, you're not doing it right. And if you're doing it well, you can identify what the fear is trying to tell you, squash it, flip it, and use it to your advantage.

Once you've gotten your fears in check, you're ready for the next-level greatness that comes with taking 100 percent responsibility.

Chapter Seven

TAKE 100 PERCENT RESPONSIBILITY

The willingness to accept responsibility for one's own life is the source from which self-respect springs.

–JOAN DIDION

IN MY EARLY THIRTIES, I DISCOVERED AN EXCEPTIONALLY USEFUL CONCEPT I've grown to love:

Take 100 percent responsibility for everything in your life—past, present, and future.

To me, it just made sense and for several reasons. Taking 100 percent responsibility removed any thought I might have about ever being a victim. And it gave me a sense of power over my circumstances I hadn't enjoyed before. If I was indeed 100 percent responsible, then I was in the position to choose all of my future results.

You might be thinking I must be crazy. One-hundred percent responsibility? Yes. Really? Yes. In every situation? Yes. In every relationship? Yes. All the time? *Yes.*

I have survived many seemingly insurmountable obstacles (I know you have, too). I can look back at each situation and am grateful for every experience and see my role in it.

I used to think that life was something that happened to me. I was navigating the ocean of life the best I could and believed I was, just as something floating in the ocean would be, at the mercy of the decisions and actions of others. Then I discovered the idea of taking 100 percent responsibility, and it caused me to reflect quite intensely on my role in each situation: the ones I was happy about, and those about which I wasn't thrilled. Initially, the concept was a tough pill to swallow! If I took 100 percent responsibility, it would mean every lousy relationship, failed business choice, job change, sour friendship, my divorce, and a laundry list of other unhappy instances was all on me. Yup. And … Yikes!

Once I embraced it, I realized I had uncovered an incredibly powerful tool I could use, now, for immediate results. Learning I was 100 percent responsible (or could choose to be if I wanted to) caused me to take ownership of all my outcomes and results. The good (I had successful businesses!), the bad (I was a divorced, single mom), and the ugly (let's just say there was some ugly, and leave it at that, okay?), all on me. 100 percent.

While I felt bummed about some of my choices, this new level of awareness promoted, among other things, a new and exciting level of achievement in all areas of my life. I have felt lighter, more efficient, and happier since I accepted this new outlook on life—not to mention, more productive. Releasing the weight of blame in my life has allowed me to become creative in astonishing ways.

Instead of choosing to feel bad about the not-so-great aspects of my choices, I choose to find the lessons and the blessings contained within them (and I will expand upon this later).

I could say *my parents acted in this way, I was and am their victim, and that's why I'm doing what I'm doing.* But the truth is I choose how I behave now, as an adult. Or, I could say *my ex-husband treated me poorly*, but the truth is, I picked him in spite of the many warning signs.

You can blame any one of more than one million events, people, places, or circumstances for your life's challenges—or you can take responsibility for your mind, thinking, feeling, behaviors, and attitude.

Which do you think will help you the most? Place blame on other causes or take responsibility and change your thinking without blaming yourself or your circumstances?

What does taking responsibility mean? It means acknowledging that you can consciously choose the outcome that is most in alignment with the vision you want to create.

Taking full responsibility for a situation means taking 100 percent responsibility with (and this is important) no fault or blame. Taking responsibility for a positive situation is easy. Think about it. When a project is a success, our first, instinctual reaction is to take all the credit (while secretly we know who REALLY made the success happen). It's not so easy to take full responsibility when you have a hot mess on your hands.

Taking full responsibility is not a trivial process. You're going to have to dig deep and get real. The path to taking 100 percent responsibility is not for the weak, yet the rewards are tremendous, and the feeling of personal freedom is entirely worth it.

Just saying, "Okay, I now take 100 percent responsibility" isn't enough. I'm providing a five-stage process to help you more effortlessly move closer to the core issue of any event:

ACKNOWLEDGE, ACCEPT, BE ACCOUNTABLE, DECIDE, AND GET RESULTS

First, choose any situation or relationship that you often find yourself reflecting on. Most likely, you're not happy with its current state or the result, or you might not be taking the time to reflect. Here's how to figure out what went wrong (and right), get past it, take responsibility, and move forward:

1. ACKNOWLEDGE THE SITUATION AND LOOK AT THE RESULT.

You might have an initial emotional reaction, and that's quite okay and perfectly normal. Everything from "D'oh! I wish that had turned out differently," or "Yuck! I can't imagine anything worse."

2. ACCEPT WHAT IS.

Yup, the situation "is what it is." You can't change it, and there's no need to try to cover it up, downplay it, or exaggerate it. This step requires further analysis of the event while adopting a detached perspective. Identify the gift or blessing in the situation (this will help with step three).

3. IDENTIFY WHO IS TRULY ACCOUNTABLE.

Ask yourself, *Who is at fault? Who is to blame?* If your answer is anyone other than "me," you have not reached the stage of accepting full accountability. This can be a difficult question to grapple with because, at first, it is hard to take ownership. No question about that! However, until you can adopt an attitude of full accountability, you cannot accept full responsibility. When you do, you will be able to get to the point where you can give thanks for what happened.

4. MAKE A DECISION.

Now you have a decision on your hands. You can choose to go into "reaction" mode and sink into a cycle of regret, resentment, and revenge, which will land you squarely in a state of guilt (not as much fun as it sounds).

This is often the instinctive, unconscious choice. I suggest you can consciously choose to move into "action." Ask yourself, "what is the positive message for me in this situation? What did I learn? What great has come, or could come, from it? The positive choice to look for the horse in a pile of shiznit takes faith at first, so of course it's harder! However, as you get used to choosing "action," it becomes easier and more natural.

5. DEFINE YOUR NEW OUTCOME.

You have two outcomes with every situation: "to grow" or "feel guilty." With full responsibility, every outcome in your life is an opportunity to grow, to live up to your potential, to get everything you want out of your life! Anything less than full responsibility sends you down the slippery slope into guilt, and guilt is just not effective.

No matter what you're doing in life, there will be situations where things feel like they are going wrong, where you've made choices that don't seem like they are turning out to be the best. It may even be that there were dishonorable intentions behind the negative impact (i.e., you were "set up" to fail). Should you choose to take full responsibility for the situation (and remember, this is always a choice), this means that you are consciously and freely choosing to say YES! to yourself.

If you are still feeling guilty about any situation, that's a signal to you that you may be accepting less than 100 percent responsibility. Take a second look at the situation that you feel guilty about, and ask how you can reframe your attitudes about the event in a way that you can understand what has happened and how it will benefit you in the future. And if you need to make amends, by all means, make them.

Full responsibility is about who has control over your life, your choices, and your results. A life of full responsibility becomes a life of amazing lightness and ease because you take full control of the outcomes in your life!

Turning an idea into reality is a very responsible step. Take anything less than 100 percent responsibility for the outcome of your idea, whether that outcome is a success or a failure, and you are cheating yourself out of the greatest joy of living. You owe it to yourself, your sanity, and your happiness to take charge of your life by taking full responsibility.

WHAT'S AWESOME ABOUT BEING 100 PERCENT RESPONSIBLE

Here is the best news: being 100 percent responsible puts you—not others—in control. It is just this control that is so attractive about 100 percent responsibility. Being in control is indeed *freedom*. The opportunities that come with it provide some real insights into what it takes to participate in and create the changes that result in dramatic improvement.

If you're addicted to drama, complaining, or—as they say in Hawaii—"talking story" (the equivalent of gossiping), taking 100 percent responsibility is going to be a new way of living for you. You will no longer call everyone you know to discuss "what happened!" or throw someone under the bus or guess what's going to happen next. You won't spend a lot of time marinating in previous conversations.

Instead, what you're talking about with yourself and others is going to be new and different. You're going to be future-focused, talking positively and about what you're creating. You've got opportunities with this shift in your mindset, and lots of them.

Here are just some of the opportunities that come with adopting an attitude of 100 percent responsibility:

OPPORTUNITIES FOR INSPIRED ACTIONS

The commitment to take 100 percent personal responsibility carries with it the opportunity for inspired actions. You can assess each area or situation and take action. You'll stop seeking permission and discover what you want to do. It changes the conversations you have with yourself (and the people in your life) from "Can I?" to "I can!" as well as "What is an effective way for me to ...?"

When you take ownership, you feel confident and with confidence comes the energy and motivation to take action.

OPPORTUNITIES TO DEFINE YOUR VISION, GOALS, AND OUTCOMES

With 100 percent responsibility comes the ability to know, and say out loud, what you are taking responsibility for and to define what a good result looks like. You will establish goals for achievement and the quality standards that will be the benchmarks for your life. And you'll share them without reservation.

OPPORTUNITIES FOR WONDERING

Taking 100 percent responsibility for your results causes a real interest in where you are putting your energy, what's working, and what isn't. Every action you take and the emotions you feel get your full attention. You wonder about them and can change them instantly when necessary.

OPPORTUNITIES TO BE POSITIVE

When you are 100 percent responsible, you look at your results carefully and are quick to give yourself grace. You know you are a good person, and you're doing the best you can. Therefore, you do not seek to judge and place blame, but to understand the relationship between what you did and your results. Results, even those that you are not happy with, are just information. You can take that information, evaluate it, and make adjustments and course corrections. Or not.

As you can see, taking 100 percent responsibility is opposed to trying too hard. When you're trying to make something happen, you're forcing the result. When you take responsibility, you're in the flow, allowing your intentions to show up, noticing what you're getting (or not), and making modifications where necessary, without pain or judgment. You're having a great time, and it shows.

START TAKING 100 PERCENT RESPONSIBILITY NOW: YOUR ACTION STEPS

Seriously, these are just a sampling of what's available to you as you shift from *trying so fucking hard* to *taking 100 percent responsibility*. The decision to start is easy, and getting great at it will take practice. Let me help by reviewing the steps above in a slightly different way.

- **Acknowledge where you are today.** Don't make your situation worse than it is, or better than it is. Just acknowledge it.

- **Now, accept it, all of it: yourself, your situation, relationships, financial status, even your age**. There isn't a darn thing you can do about the past. Accepting it will set you free!

   Say "I am fully accountable for this situation." (Again, it is what it is!)

- **Decide to change the future.** Draw a line in the sand and commit to doing whatever it takes to get your desired results.

What are the visions and goals you want to bring to fruition? Sit down and have a field day imagining your goals and visions, then go next level and imagine them as achieved. Know this: your life will exactly be like you imagine it because you have the power to create it.

Combine your new commitment to taking 100 percent responsibility with your incredible attitude and watch the magic that happens next! Taking ownership of how you respond, instead of reacting, is a significant factor in determining results. Whether you see the glass as half-full or half-empty does make a difference in your ultimate outcomes. Decide to take 100 percent responsibility and full ownership of your life and the outcomes you desire.

Ask empowering, positively-phrased questions, such as "What is the most effective way to move forward?" or "How can I lose weight/start a business/find the love of my life and enjoy the process?" to encourage creativity and effective problem-solving. Your answer is almost always determined by the question, and when you ask a great question, you will get a great answer.

Let's take 100 percent responsibility up a tiny notch: put the words and energy of "blame" and "victim" in the off-limits category. Eliminate them from your vocabulary, don't give anyone else the blame, and be clear about the fact you are never a victim. If you find yourself in a situation you don't like, it is okay. You chose it, and now you can un-choose it, or choose to make changes. You "chose in" and you can "choose out." What happens next is entirely up to you.

Those who choose to adopt 100 percent responsibility experience sustainable internal and external balance, have more energy, are more excited about life, and overall, they are happier. But just in case you're still not convinced that 100 percent responsibility is for you, here are a few more benefits.

MORE ABOUT WHAT'S AWESOME ABOUT BEING 100 PERCENT RESPONSIBLE

100 percent responsibility will have a profound impact on your ability to create and maintain successful, aligned, and more effective personal and professional relationships—all of which will lead to your increased satisfaction and overall happiness.

You now have a healthy alternative to the blaming and victim roles that greatly escalate the conflict and impede relationship (and life) effectiveness and happiness! 100 percent responsibility involves joining with others in the ownership for results, rather than personalizing or blaming.

100 percent responsibility provides a way of approaching potentially difficult situations in ways that are clean and clarifying. Challenging situations will be resolved while rapport is increased. You will be more attractive to yourself, making you irresistible to others.

You'll eliminate negative and unproductive conversations. Imagine having most of your conversations focused on "what's next" and "what are you creating?" and "how can I support and assist you?" Commit to yourself to notice what conversations you're having and shift them to the positive—even mid-sentence if necessary.

I can promise you a level of peace and happiness you might not have experienced in quite some time, if ever, by taking 100 percent responsibility. If this concept resonates with you, then you're going to love our discussion in the next chapter.

Remember:

Pain is inevitable. Suffering is optional.
—ANONYMOUS

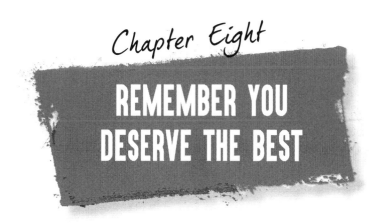

Chapter Eight

REMEMBER YOU DESERVE THE BEST

You deserve the best.

—UNKNOWN

IF YOU'VE SPENT YOUR LIFE TRYING TOO FUCKING HARD, chances are you've bent over backward and repeatedly gone the extra mile to make sure someone you care about (and sometimes someone you don't) got the very best. You've probably sacrificed your happiness, money, or time to provide the best for someone else, even when it was highly inconvenient for you.

That's very nice of you. Well done. Giving to others is wonderful and amazing, and I'm sure you were appreciated. At least I hope so.

Now stop it. At least stop it for other people until you give yourself the best with the same vim and vigor with which you've given to others.

When I first became a business coach more than twenty years ago, I discovered the tenets of coaching. Among them: **Become Incredibly Selfish** is one of my favorites.

At first the word *selfish* put me back on my heels. I mean, *Webster's* dictionary defines selfish as "caring unduly or supremely for oneself; regarding one's comfort, advantage, etc., in disregard, or at the expense of, that of others."

I mean, narcissistic much? Upon further investigation, I grew to love this idea.

Now, in my mind, being selfish is an integral part of being good to myself. Being good to myself means I'm giving myself the best. When I give myself the best, I am the best I can be for myself and everyone else. I know you want to be your best, and as you begin to choose the best for yourself, you will be able to.

Stay with me here—indeed for the sake of your personal and professional happiness and success, you would be well-served to view selfishness in a new and wonderful way. If you don't like the word selfish, upgrade it to self-*full*—self-fullness means filling up your soul and yourself *from the inside*. Which is precisely what giving yourself the best does, it allows you to feel full—be full—without anything external.

Fortune favors the bold and brave, and the bold and the brave are guided by their own light. Giving yourself the best allows you to be your highest and best self, and ultimately enables you to be more generous and supportive of others than you could have been before. It's you, only not just better, but *best*. You're lit up from within, and it shows.

BENEFITS OF GIVING YOURSELF THE BEST

When you give yourself the best, when you learn to practice Supreme Self-Care consistently, many wonderful things begin to happen in your life. Up until now, you've been trying too fucking hard, which means you haven't exhaled since, well, forever. It's time for an upgrade; trust me on this one.

You've put everyone else first. Now, as you start putting yourself first, you will have less stress and less sickness, and in their place will go health, happiness, and a sense of calm and well-being.

Those who give tend to have to keep on giving. Others who have relied on you (instead of themselves) have no reservation about taking until you have nothing left. Downshift into taking care of yourself, while simultaneously holding others capable of finding a solution (or someone else for them to rely on).

When you give yourself the best, you won't need as much from others as you may have in the past. Giving yourself the best means getting what you truly need, when you need it. When you meet your needs, you don't need as much from others (up to and including their approval).

You stop doing without, and you have more of what you want and need, more of the time.

I'm going to help you make the connection between what is best for you and how to get it. Upgrading isn't as hard as you might think, and you can get started right away.

Allow me to reiterate, just as in the previous chapter, that when you are feeling and doing your best, it doesn't only benefit you. You at your highest, best, and happiest makes you a better human for yourself and everyone else. You are a better parent, child, friend, neighbor, business person, driver, and citizen.

At the top of the list, pun intended, is putting yourself first. Surely you've traveled by airplane, and every flight begins with a safety presentation that includes *Put the oxygen mask on yourself before you assist someone else.*

Putting yourself first—heck, putting yourself on your list for possibly the first time—is going to ensure you get the results you've ultimately been trying to get the whole time. Without trying so fucking hard!

In case you're not entirely convinced, some of the other benefits include:

More than enough. With great self-care practices, you can build a reserve in every area of life that matters. There is nothing like having an abundance of everything you need, right when you need it. Ever spilled coffee down your shirt five minutes before you have to leave for a meeting? Having an extra shirt comes in handy. Building a reserve of time, money, space, love, and whatever else you'd like to have an abundance of is a fun game, and the benefits are unparalleled!

A reserve of time lessens stress and prevents the need to feel rushed or in a hurry. If you're always late, focus on building in extra time for everything on your calendar. Go to bed a few minutes early so you can journal, talk to your spouse, or read a few additional pages in that book you've been meaning to finish. Try getting up fifteen minutes earlier so you can enjoy the paper and a fresh cup of coffee before the kids get up (or a Miracle Morning practice).

A reserve of money allows for handling unexpected expenses without distress, or, on the flip side, the opportunity to be generous when needed. You'll love being able to afford no-strings-attached generosity, capitalizing on a great investment, or buying exactly what you want.

A reserve of personal energy and self-respect. Saying *no* any time you'd like. Being able to say no to a job, project, or client because you would rather do something (anything!) else is a joy.

Saying *yes* any time you'd like. Saying yes to opportunities and anything that sounds like a good time is also pretty great.

Bonus: a reserve of self-knowledge and understanding. Learn what you like and what you don't. Do more of what you want and less (or none) of what you don't.

You'll be sure, as a positive by-product, to increase your self-esteem and what you know you deserve. The better you treat yourself, the better you'll treat yourself! It's easy to get addicted to feeling great, and when you feel great, you want to keep feeling great. The process is akin to an upward trajectory you will love and won't want to do without.

Rather than being in a downward spiral, you'll find yourself in a positive upward spiral. The more reserves you build, the more opportunities to build a reserve show up. I've been on a downward spiral, and those are no fun. Upward spirals are fun, and it takes just a little intention to get them started and focus on keeping them going.

PUTTING THE BEST FOR YOURSELF *INTO PRACTICE*

Giving yourself the best, adopting the practice of Supreme Self-Care, will require you to look at different aspects of your life and deciding what the best looks like *for you*.

Here are ten areas you'll want to look at, and there are dozens of other possibilities you can add on:

1. Your Emotions

2. Your Personal Environments

3. Your Intimate Circle, Inner Circle, and Everyone Else

4. Your Well-Being

5. Your Dream Team

6. Your Fuel

7. Your Appearance

8. Your Sustainability

9. Your Rituals for Happiness and Success

10. Your Miscellaneous Needs

YOUR EMOTIONS

As I've mentioned, and I'm sure you can relate, when I'm not my best, I can't be my best for myself or others. Lack of sleep or food (or the right food), with an increase in stress (good or bad) does not allow us to put our best foot forward or create our desired results.

I suggest you focus not on lowering your stress, but on eliminating it. A radical approach, it's true, but one I've done on a few occasions in varying degrees of intensity. Every single time (every one!), I've been glad I've made the changes I've made. Focus solely on reducing your stress, and you may not even notice a difference. Changing the scenario entirely can be a game-changer.

- Maybe what you're doing for a living is making you rich but killing your soul. If you can't eliminate the stress with some great coaching, compelling questions, and thoughtful adjustments, change your position, resign, or switch careers.

- Outsource everything you don't love to do, and use automatic services in every possible way (such as bill pay, grocery delivery, automatic deposit or withdrawal).

- Delegate every task you don't do for a living (such as housekeeping, legal work or tax prep, and errand running).

YOUR PERSONAL ENVIRONMENTS

Without question, we are products of our environments—past and present. What you might not realize is you have the opportunity to adapt or completely redesign your environments to serve you in the best possible way.

- I believe your home should rise up to meet you. In other words, decorated to your taste, and have only the people, pets, and things within it you love. When you awaken in the morning or re-enter your home after any length of absence, it is vital for you to feel pinch-me happy. A peaceful and nurturing home environment will allow you to recharge and draw energy from which to take on just about anything.

- Have a place for everything, use with care and in good health, and return everything to its place. Being organized is peaceful and a stress reducer. Give yourself the gift of a stress-free environment by being neat and organized.

- My office is in my home (and in various neighborhood coffee shops). When I had a spare room to use as an office, I fancied it up completely. I had chairs for visitors, plants for clean air, snacks and beverages handy, and it was organized and efficient, inspiring and pretty. While I have no need these days for dedicated office space, I highly recommend you make wherever you work fit you to a "T." Whether you have a mobile, home, or outside office, tailor it to you and what you need to work optimally.

YOUR INTIMATE CIRCLE, INNER CIRCLE, AND EVERYONE ELSE

Widely-respected motivational speaker Jim Rohn once said, "You're the average of the five people with whom you spend most of your time." It is, however, common to underestimate the importance of the company you keep. Bottom line: The people around you matter.

We all need people: family, friends, colleagues, mentors and more who will challenge us and make us better. The people closest to us either hold us back, raise us up, or help us maintain a continual pursuit of higher standards.

If you're the smartest person in the room, you're in the wrong room! Surround yourself as much and often as possible with people who can run circles around you in whatever area you need improvement.

I classify the people in my life into three categories:

- My Intimate Circle. My intimate circle consists of my closest family members, including my husband, daughter, and a few others. It also includes my closest friends. In one way or another, I'm in contact with them often, if not every day.

- My inner circle. My inner circle is full of people I stay in touch with on a regular basis. We may not connect more than a couple of times a month, but we're close.

- Everyone else. Anyone not in the above two groups, no matter how we're related to each other, or how I know them or for how long.

Why three groups and what are the differences?

Well, when I need support or encouragement, to hide a body (just kidding! Are you really reading this?), have an ugly cry, or borrow money, I'm going to work my way through my intimate and inner circles. If something really cool happens (I hit a goal, such as finish a book), those are the folks I call. These are the folks who are closest to me, and we rely on each other to enjoy our spins around the sun.

Then, there's everyone else. These are also the folks for whom I haven't a fuck to give about their opinion. Remember the #ZeroFucks T-shirt? I have learned, *the hard way*, that giving too much weight to someone's opinion (good, bad, or indifferent) when they should not even necessarily have an opinion is not good. In fact, it's terrible.

I now use a neat little trick whenever I receive either a compliment or a criticism: I say thank you and give each equal weight.

- If someone says I'm the most amazing person they've ever met, I say, *Thank you!* And I go on about my day, same as before. I mean how could they know if I am or I'm not? I could be a freakin' serial killer (but don't worry, I'm not).

- Same with criticism. I've been called all sorts of horrible things in my life. I give the same response: *Thank you.* Then I get on with my day. I could be Mother Theresa reincarnated. They just really don't know, now do they?

Their opinion is based on, most likely, just a few data points of information. If they like me, but don't *know* me, they have no idea about my morals, daily actions, or standards, or whether I am truly good or bad. Therefore, their opinion does not matter.

I give equal weight to both perspectives because I don't think it's healthy to have a great day because a stranger tells me I'm terrific, or a horrible day because they think I'm worse than the grandmother who used to make them sleep in the barn. They don't know, so what they think can't matter if I want to keep my sanity. And I do. And so do you, I would imagine.

This section is extra-long because too often I see people giving a lot of weight to what other people think and say about them, and it ruins everything from an hour to several decades. Take back your power by determining who you're going to have in your intimate and inner circles, and then let everyone else go about their business while you go about yours.

In the meantime, evaluate who you've got in your life right now and consider cleaning some house, if necessary. You can also identify some gems in the third group and give them an upgrade at any time.

Here's the tough part: doing a silent critique of the people you keep around you. This may sound judgmental or downright ruthless but understanding the influence they have on your overall mood, and general performance is critical to your success. You simply have too much at stake to let this go unaddressed. If someone is bringing down your average, you have to reduce their involvement in your life (or eliminate them entirely by moving them to the "everyone else" column). Failure to make necessary adjustments is expensive (too expensive to ignore)! It will hinder your energy, health, and ultimately, your happiness and success. You can't afford it, no matter how rich you might be.

Write down a list of the major players in your life, and classify them as Intimate Circle, Inner Circle, and Everyone Else.

This won't just make the holidays a more manageable and less stressful time (fewer gifts to buy, more joy and laughter), it will help you stay close and deepen the relationships that matter.

Benjamin Hardy, author of *Willpower Doesn't Work,* recently did an article about how to use the iPhone audio text message feature to develop deep and meaningful relationships. Used on your own time, you can send a voice message (think voicemail without the incessant ringing) anytime you'd like—and the recipient can get it and listen to it at their convenience.

Since I read that article (you can read it here: https://tinyurl.com/BHPhoneText), I've been a voice-texting fool. I've sent messages to my mother-in-law, future son-in-law (you know who you are), assistant, daughter, husband, and tons of friends. It's enjoyable and fun. I send messages from in the car, on the treadmill, while I'm making dinner (thank you, AirPods). When I think about someone now, I send them a voice text. I'm really enjoying the benefits of connecting with people, and it's fun to hear, "I really enjoyed hearing your voice."

Let's turn our focus to you and your closest relationships. I would imagine you're reading this book because you're at least a smidgen frustrated with one relationship in your life. If that's the case, well, it only takes one relationship to completely take us off-kilter, slow our roll, and leave us on the wrong side of success.

Let's first do an inventory, and then analyze it for some possible changes or upgrades.

YOUR FIVE.

Who are the five people you spend the most time with (as referenced above)? Picture each of them individually while considering the following:

- Are they adding value to your life?
- Do they make you feel great?

- Are the conversations they start with you mostly focused on problems or problem-solving?

- When you're about to see them, do you feel a positive emotion or a negative one?

- Based on your answers, are they an asset or a liability?

What if you don't have five? Believe me when I say, *Less can be more!* If you only have one person on whom you can rely in this lifetime, consider yourself blessed. Relationships and friendships—intimate and personal—can last a lifetime. They can exist for a reason or a season.

What if you have more than five? You can consider yourself an incredibly blessed being, and I suggest you spend a few minutes daily counting those blessings (and by all means, send them a voice text soon!).

WHO ARE YOU IN EACH RELATIONSHIP?

Now, as you picture each person, ask the same questions but in reverse.

- Are you adding value to their life?

- Do you make them feel great?

- Are the conversations you start with them mostly focused on problems or problem-solving?

- When they are about to see you, do they feel a positive emotion or a negative one?

- Based on your answers, are you an asset or a liability?

I don't think it's too much to ask for the majority of my inner circle interactions to be great! I want my most significant relationships to give me the warm fuzzies, a soft place to land, and unending love, support, and encouragement. And that's my goal for each of them as well.

WHAT DO YOU WANT, AND DO YOU HAVE IT?

It is important to get clear about what you want in each of your significant relationships. It is okay to ask for what you want and to get it!

If you have five solid close relationships, you can probably skip this next section. But if your initial evaluation has left you wanting more: more valued connections or a deeper connection with any of your current relationships, I have a few suggestions.

LOOK WITHIN.

I distinctly remember my first-grade teacher saying, *To have a friend you must be a friend.* I'm going to dive more deeply into my philosophy in the next chapter. For now, suffice it to say, if you want a friend, find someone and be their friend. Figure out who you need to become to be the kind of person who has quality relationships and focus on you.

Be cognizant of who you are helping, inspiring and holding to a higher standard—and vice versa! The best relationships are symbiotic in which both bring out the best in one another. How can you do a better job or what value can you add to others' lives? You want to be instrumental in bringing them up!

BE OPEN TO CHANGE.

As you grow, your five people may evolve or even change. Your five closest friends in high school are probably very different than your five today. You probably didn't have to throw out those high school friends—their roles evolved naturally over time. You don't need to escort someone to the door. If you determine someone is toxic, lose touch with them over time. Aren't you sometimes too busy to talk to your BFF? Well then, you're certainly too busy to talk to the person who is always giving a back-handed compliment or making you feel like you don't measure up. Send them to voicemail, leave their texts unanswered, and get on with your day!

True friendships endure, especially when you have a focus on growing them. As you're merely focusing your valuable time most effectively for you, some relationships will naturally run their course. Conversely, if there are people who you think will help you improve, make a concerted effort to spend more time with them.

YOUR WELL-BEING

What is well-being and how do you get yours? Well-being is the state of being, well, *well*. Positive psychology refers to it as "authentic happiness." I like to think of having enough of everything I need when I need it— and a little extra (just in case), as well as being in the flow. For me, it means I can write when I need to write, coach when I need to coach, be fully present whether I'm at dinner with my family or getting a pedicure with my daughter and mother-in-law. All while I'm healthy, happy, and well-rested.

Stop trying so fucking hard and place some emphasis on your well-being. I practice yoga, workout consistently, and regularly get haircuts, facials, and massages. I take naps, go to bed early most of the time, read as much as I can, and spend lots of free time with my family and friends.

When I neglect to do any of the above, wow, what a difference. No, none of them are *necessary*. But after many years of trial and error, I've found my well-being allows me to contribute to the well-being of others. And I have the bandwidth to do it, which makes a huge difference.

Engaging a team of health-care professionals is one of the best investments you can make. Think the above list is indulgent? Think again—consider taking great care of yourself the best maintenance plan of your most valuable asset: you.

Living at your highest possible level of well-being pays off in big and little ways over time: you're healthier, more productive, more constructive, and more creative. Just for starters!

Convinced? Oh good—here are some suggestions to boost your well-being:

- Live in the here and now. Stop straining and striving and chasing, enjoy each moment as it arrives. Jesse

Itzler, author of *Living with the Monks,* suggests monotasking—true focus on one thing at a time.

- Cultivate great health with regular medical and dental check-ups, including blood work and exams. Taking great care of yourself is just good personal business.

- Exercise regularly. Find something you love so much you look forward to doing it as often as possible! Next level: find a workout buddy or tribe of folks focused on fitness.

Start with these, as I did, and see where you end up. Chances are you'll love your new routine so much you'll expand it in a way suited perfectly to your lifestyle.

In the meantime, you'll need to keep your cup full, even as you transition to a new, happy normal. Look for opportunities to do "mini fill-ups." You might be struggling to find just a few extra minutes in your day. I understand. Identify what you can do to fill your cup in one-, five-, and ten-minute increments. It just takes one minute to step outside for some fresh air. Identify a quick mantra to ground you and say it while sitting at your desk or during a swift trip to the restroom. You might be able to take a quick ten-minute walk around the block or steal away to enjoy a cup of hot tea. Post your list on the fridge, bathroom mirror, or leave a copy on your desk. Set an alarm or reminder timer to do one of them every hour of the day.

YOUR DREAM TEAM

Execute your Supreme Self-care by investing in experts to maximize each aspect of your life. Consider yourself the sole elite athlete on your team, and you need a supporting cast to keep yourself in top form. You may not need all of the folks listed below, but a strong bench makes for a winning team.

You can:

- Work with a personal coach if you are challenged with your friendships, personal boundaries, and/or have goals you want to achieve.

- Engage a fantastic business coach. They are worth multiples what you'll pay them for their sage advice and guidance. The right coach will help you make more money in less time, eliminate obstacles, and help you get where you're going faster and with less effort. (I know, I used to be one and still have one!).

- Work with a therapist to keep your mental health in order. We all benefit from help with healing old wounds and navigating current daily challenges.

- Work with a chiropractor or bodyworker to keep your musculoskeletal system in tip-top shape and remove energy blocks.

- Have a weekly or twice-monthly massage, the benefits of which include relaxation and recovery, as well as fulfilling one's regular need for touch.

- A dermatologist can thoroughly examine your skin to ensure you don't have any unwanted maladies, and an aesthetician can keep you looking great.

- A personal attorney and a business attorney are worth their weight in gold. In your lifetime, you will need a will, living will, powers of attorney for different situations, as well as agreements, engagement letters, and contracts for business situations.

- Eliminate all monetary concerns by developing relationships with a banker, bookkeeper, certified public accountant, financial advisor, and insurance agent. Having stable relationships with experts who know you and your situation well can and will come in handy many times over.

YOUR FUEL

A year after I met my mother-in-law, she said, "The difference between you and me is that you eat to live, and I live to eat, which is why you're so much healthier than I am!"

I don't think my way of eating is the only way or the best way. It is the only and best way *for me*. Through trial and error, I've learned what to ingest to keep me running like a well-oiled machine (tons of water, lean meats, vegetables, eggs, and an avocado a day … and of course, coffee and herbal tea), and what to avoid or else (processed foods, anything with lots of sugar, and alcohol). Of course, the former list is dull as all get out, and the latter is delicious and tempting but also not great *for me*.

I don't have to stick to my best food program, but when I do, I'm the better for it. But I'm human after all, and girlfriend here loves pizza and a 7-layer chocolate cake as much as the next person. I've learned to apply the 80/20 Rule to my diet: eighty percent of the time I eat like an Olympic athlete and twenty percent of the time, I could challenge you to, and win, a cupcake-eating contest.

Everything in moderation.

I suggest you play around with different foods and drinks and figure out what helps you to be your best, and what you might want to let go of, stop doing, or do less.

YOUR APPEARANCE

Oscar Wilde once wrote, *It is only shallow people who do not judge by appearances.* Taking care of your outside as well as your inside is an integral part of Supreme Self-Care.

When you look good, you feel good. Although it takes extra time, I attempt to look my best every day for several reasons. One, because I feel great when I look my best. Second, I never know when I'm going to run into someone (homeless is not a good look). Finally, more than twice I've needed to run out of the house and not being dressed or having had a shower would have been highly inconvenient at the least and be embarrassing at the most.

Here's your cheat sheet for always looking awesome:

- Only have clothing that fits you *right now* (not for a weight you were or are planning to be), makes you look great, and suits your personality and body type.

  Next level: have a capsule, minimalist wardrobe— grown-up Garanimals (where all of the clothes can be mixed and matched). Purging your closet, defining your style, and keeping only the items you truly love, and wear will minimize the amount of time you need to pull yourself together. Just twenty-five items can create dozens of effortless outfits that have you out the door in no time.

- Have your hair cut and styled (and colored) exactly the way you like it.

- Get regular manicures and pedicures. My husband, after his first pedicure, said, "These are amazing! Why haven't I been getting them the whole time?" It is common for men to get manicures and pedicures, now more than ever!

- Have unwanted hair? With just a few treatments over a couple of months, you can get it re-moved forever.

- Have (or give yourself) a monthly facial. Not only are they great for your skin, but they are also Supreme Self-Care at the highest level. Taking great care of your skin is also a way to stay looking and feeling youthful and vibrant.

- Wear only the best, most comfortable and fabulous shoes you can find. I've become obsessed with Rothy's (which are made from recycled plastic bottles and made with a 3D printer! Cool, right?), which are stylish and keep me comfortably on my feet for hours on end.

- Get and keep your body in excellent shape. Focus on your cardio health, strength, and flexibility and your 100-year-old self will thank you!

- Get regular teeth cleanings to keep your dental and overall health in tip-top shape, find the humor in all you can, and smile at every opportunity.

YOUR SUSTAINABILITY

Everything I've talked about thus far is meant to be a permanent addition to your lifestyle and natural behavior, not just a temporary effort.

You'll also find it helpful to:

- Structure finances to eliminate all financial concerns, so money or cost doesn't drive decisions.

- Work through childhood issues, so they don't show up at inopportune moments or affect current behavior, in addition to resolving any damage as it happens.

- Say no early and often.

- Know your strengths and install support and systems to do what you can't, won't, or don't do for yourself.

There's a lot in those few bullet points. Just focusing on those four will help you live at a level that has joy in every day and almost no stress.

YOUR DAILY RITUALS

Supreme Self-Care is a daily process, not just a one-time action. Here are a few best practices I use daily and think you'll love, too:

- Stretching. Or yoga. Keeping yourself flexible as well as in good shape will mean you'll enjoy good health for as long as you live.

- Morning Ritual. Check out *The Miracle Morning* book series, which includes a six-step ritual guaranteed to transform your life, one morning at a time.

- Brush and floss twice a day. Add in a Waterpik and your dentist will consider you a star patient.

- Spend your days, *all of them*, doing what you want to do.

- Remember to say *no*.

- Under-promise always, and overdeliver whenever you can.

- Have something to look forward to every day.

- Pre-schedule breaks, naps, days just for fun, and regular vacations.

- If you're an introvert, schedule alone time to recharge (daily); if you're an extrovert, schedule time with others (daily or as needed).

- Talk to a friend and a family member at least once a day. Studies show the happiest people are those with wonderful relationships.

- Bedtime Ritual. I start "powering down" about ninety minutes before I want to fall asleep. Either a quick shower or a long, warm bath, with some hot tea and reading, ending with a guided meditation (via the Pzizz app) allows me to fall asleep, on time, and with a smile on my face.

None of these daily rituals will take up a ton of your time, but they add so much value, time, and a sense of calm and happiness to you and your life. You'll want to add your own as you discover them.

YOUR MISCELLANEOUS NEEDS–SPECIAL CARE GOES HERE!

When I got my divorce, I discovered one of my needs quite by accident. My therapist and coach, in the same week, recommended I read *The Five Love Languages* by Gary Chapman. When you're courting, you usually meet your mate's needs by fulfilling all five of the love languages (words of affirmation, acts of service, receiving gifts, quality time, and physical touch). In the beginning, both parties are saying and doing everything the other person needs. After we settle into a relationship, we settle into the primary and secondary love languages that work best for us. It turns out, this is a huge mistake and can lead to a break-up.

As I found myself a single mom after seven years of marriage, both my coach and therapist wanted to ensure

I was as healthy as I wanted to be, then as a single woman, and in the future in a new relationship.

What I discovered was that my top two love languages are quality time and physical touch. That second one can be quite problematic, if not addressed in a wise and healthy way. I was single, and a single mom, but I needed physical touch to operate at my best. Hmmm.

My coach suggested weekly massage, which changed my life. Without boring you with the entire story, I was able to make clear-headed relationship decisions because I didn't fall for the first guy who rubbed me the right way. (Know what I mean?)

All of this to say, you have needs, and there is nothing wrong with having them! Identify them and meet them in a healthy and constructive way (so they are *not met* in an unhealthy and destructive way).

Make a list of your special needs, wants, and desires—the ones you haven't seen elsewhere in this book or chapter. Use your imagination and be very specific. Next to each need, write several positive and constructive ways you can get your need met (and if you're feeling spunky, get a few of them on your calendar). If you're having trouble figuring out what *your* love languages are, think about the times you have felt loving toward another person. What did you do? Write them poems? Clean their house for them? Give them a massage? Bring them presents and tokens of affection? Make sure to spend time with them, arranging special outings or things you knew they'd love to do? How you spend your loving energy on others is how you like to receive love too.

You deserve the best, if only because you're a living, breathing human on this planet. This chapter has provided dozens of ways for you to stop trying so fucking hard and give yourself the best of everything. You and the world are going to be all the better for it.

I'm going to close this chapter with a little something from Oprah. Just a few days ago, right on time to help me add a little something extra to this book, I saw a video of Oprah talking about friendships—which ones to keep and which ones to kick to the curb.

Allow me to quote directly from the source:

I've had to do a clearing in my life of some people whose energy, I realized, was not supportive of who I wanted to be in the world. And I recognized there were some people who would not take responsibility for their energy and so I had to take responsibility for the energy I allow to be brought into my space. Life-changing for me. What I know is, that you cannot continue to move forward in your life, to the level and level and level that you need to be if you're surrounded by energy that brings you down, that sucks the life force from you. So not only are you responsible for the energy that you bring, what I learned, but also the energy you surround yourself with. Huge, huge, huge, huge. And everybody who is watching me right now, you know there are some energy suckers in our life, just literally taking the life force out of you and you will never be able to be and do whoever you're supposed to be and do in the world as long as you continued to buy into the energy suckers.

You might think it would be easy for Oprah to have her pick of friends, and easy for her to get rid of the ones who don't suit her, and you wouldn't be wrong. But if you think you're any different, that's where you might want to reconsider how powerful you are, and how attractive you'll be to so many people once you're owning it!

When you like yourself, and it shows, you have all of the friendships you could want.

If you want to speed the process along, I've got something waiting for you in the next chapter.

Chapter Nine

IF YOU WANT SOMETHING, GIVE IT AWAY!

Anyone who says money doesn't buy you happiness clearly hasn't given enough of it away.

—UNKNOWN

IF THE LAST CHAPTER LEFT YOU INSPIRED TO GIVE YOURSELF the best, well, then, YAY! That makes me deliriously happy. You can't go wrong with expanding your self-care and how you allow others to care for you. Now, you might be wondering how to attract some of those things into your life, without having to try too hard (*obviously*).

I've got you covered on this one. In fact, this might be my favorite share of the entire book.

My philosophy includes the tenet, *If you want something, give it away.*

This has been part of the philosophy I started developing in my early twenties. There are several, but this particular idea goes well with another one: *Leave everyone and everything better than you found them.* Not just tenets, they are personal rules I developed while I was living in New York City in the early '90s.

I've always been curious about what works and what doesn't. For as long as I can remember, I've tried to reverse engineer just about everything, so I could get the best results with the least amount of effort and in the shortest amount of time.

Enter "giving to get." Not a new concept for sure—my research for this book revealed even a Bible verse that supports it: *Give to everyone who asks you* (Luke 6:30). I'm sure we all heard *If you want to have a friend, be a friend* as far back as we can remember. I can remember hearing it in Mrs. Structner's first-grade class at East Elementary in Athens, Ohio way back in 1976. You may know it as the law of reciprocity, defined as "a social norm of responding to a positive action with another positive action."

As a business coach, I would often suggest that my clients ask probing and interesting questions when networking, then wait to see if the person they were with either did the same or talked only about themselves. Not only is it a good way to determine someone's underlying character, but it is also a quick way to figure out if you want to create a reciprocal relationship.

Giving with the expectation of receiving is not a new concept for sure—but is it front of mind for you? Do you consciously think about it? Most importantly, do you use it in your daily life to get more of what you want?

First, let's define what "it" is.

It is (1) *what you want* combined with (2) *intentionally giving it away.*

Let's start with what you want more of: time, love, money, joy, friendship, business, power, fun, laughter, *hugs*?

Pull out your journal and make a list. If you want more of something, anything, it means you don't have as much as you want right now. It might surprise you that the fastest way to get more is to give more. Legitimately, if you want something, figure out how to give it away. *Pronto.*

The very next thought you should have, once you realize you want something you don't have at all, or you want more of, is *How do I give it away, right away?* Because it's true: what you put out there comes right back to you.

THE REALIZATION THAT CHANGED MY LIFE

Every author wants book reviews, lots of them, and we prefer them to be glowing 5-star reviews. The Number One way people find their next book to read is through personal recommendation, followed by a third-party review on a major retail platform (ahem). I was lamenting my lack of book reviews one day when I had a moment of realization: *I wanted something I didn't have. So, how could I give it away?*

Here's what I came up with:

- I'm a voracious reader, and I read at least two or three books every week.

- I wasn't taking the time to leave reviews for my fellow authors. Insert "oh no!" face here! I wanted something I wasn't giving away. Oops!

- Question: *How could I give reviews away?* I committed to leave a review for any and every book I read or listened to for which I could honestly leave a 4- or 5-star review, starting with the very next book.

That very next book just happened to be *The Miracle Morning* by Hal Elrod.

The book validated a morning practice I had started in 2003, which was to spend time listening to one of the inspirational and motivational programs I had in my library and taking notes, followed by affirmations and a good workout. I was struck by Hal's story and even thought, *I could've written this book, except his "tough times" story is way cooler than mine.* (If you haven't read it, by all means grab a copy.)

What happened next is a perfect example of this idea in action. On June 19, 2013, I wrote the following review for *The Miracle Morning* on Amazon and Goodreads:

> *Miracle Morning is an excellent book. I've long practiced an AM Routine, in fact, I've shared it with my clients for years. The Miracle Morning is my AM Routine on steroids, it's going to cause me to up my game {and yours, too, if you know me}. Great job, Hal!*

On August 6, Hal saw my review and sent me an email. After a discussion with Ryan Snow about turning *The Miracle Morning* into a series and after "looking me up" to see I had written a successful series (*The Successful Single Mom* book series) he suggested we discuss a collaboration on *The Miracle Morning for Single Moms.*

We had that discussion—it lasted two hours, and by the time we were through, had decided to collaborate on what would become the second book in *The Miracle Morning* book series: *The Miracle Morning for Salespeople* with co-author Ryan Snow. We ended up doing that book, as well as two others, within the first two years. The rest, as they say, is history.

You might be reading this book because you discovered me through Hal (and if so, thank you and thank you, Hal!). In fact, we've most recently published the 13th in the series, *Miracle Morning Millionaires*, and the 14th as well, *The Miracle Morning for Addiction Recovery.*

Joining Hal to produce this series not only enriched my life with new, dear friends, I've also become a better writer, marketer, and businesswoman. And so much more.

While it is impossible to predict exactly how this principle could enrich your life, there are definite benefits from inserting this practice into your daily life.

YOU ARE GOING TO FEEL GREAT!

I don't know about you but receiving pales in comparison to giving. I am always in a conundrum after finding the perfect gift and can hardly wait until the appropriate time (a birthday or holiday) to present it to the recipient. You are going to feel amazing every time you do something for someone else, even if you do it anonymously.

YOU WILL IMPACT OTHERS IN BEAUTIFUL AND UNEXPECTED WAYS.

Keep in mind if you need something, there is someone else who needs it, too. Hugging is a prime example—we need at least eight hugs a day for optimal health and to help heal all sorts of maladies, including loneliness, anxiety, and stress. Hugs are an instant "give to get" example, and I guarantee someone around you needs one as much as you do.

Whatever you need, in fact, is needed by another human close to you. Even if you don't have much to give, you enact the law of reciprocity by priming the pump with your giving.

Struggling financially or want to expand your reserves? Go for a drive, find a homeless person and give them some money (and a cold bottle of water and a sandwich). Or, send a monetary gift to someone on your team.

Feeling depressed or lonely? Head to a senior center and ask to the speak to the old man who hasn't had a visitor in forever.

As I write this, two major celebrities have recently committed suicide, Kate Spade and Anthony Bourdain. While someone may not be that far down when you extend an unexpected kindness, *everyone* is dealing with challenges others know nothing about, and you never know when your giving will make someone's day or save their life. Be sure to check in on your strong and positive friends, as they need it, too.

YOU'LL CREATE WIN-WINS LIKE YOU'VE NEVER SEEN BEFORE!

As in my case with Hal, sometimes giving comes with an unexpected collaboration or partnership. I don't expect anything in return when I give, but I am always in a state of positive expectation—I know more is coming my way and I'm ready for it!

Oh, and sometimes the win-win you're a party to doesn't involve you at all. I like to ask, *What do you need right now?* in almost every conversation. Sometimes the answer is *A two-hour nap and $8 million,* and sometimes it's a gift I can give. On several occasions, I've been asked, "Who do you know who …" and I've been able to make an introduction. It is great fun to make connections, and those connections have resulted in marriages, employment, home sales, and so much more.

UNEXPECTED MAGIC AND MIRACLES *WILL HAPPEN* FOR YOU!

One of my mentors used a farming analogy to explain his view on the world (and specifically our business), *When you're plowing the front 20, the back 80 is popping up.* Said another way, sometimes you're reaping in a place other than where you're sowing. Chalk it up to good karma points or whatever you'd like, but as you are doing good, there is good on your path. Seeds don't always bloom where we plant them, but they do bloom eventually nonetheless.

I believe we can't out-give the universe. If I do you a favor, and you blow me off, I'm still good! I know I'm racking up good karma points with every positive deed. I know it won't be long before I'm the recipient of some serious awesomeness.

PUT IT IN ACTION

I bet if you haven't before, you're anxious to put this into action. I don't blame you—the fun is in the giving, although the receiving is pretty darn sweet, too.

You can start small—pre-pay for someone's coffee the next time you visit Starbucks or give an extra-large tip to the high school kid delivering pizzas. Greet your check-out gal at the grocery store by name and thank her for her smile. Ask for help to your car and slip a five-dollar tip to your helper.

The next time you're hungry, don't eat alone. Call a friend you haven't seen in a while and ask them to join you for a last-minute lunch. If they accept, treat. If they don't, probe for a future date when you can. Be sure to leave an extra few bucks in your server's tip, especially if they're terrific.

The bottom line is: figure out what you want and figure out how to give it away as soon and as often as possible.

I'll leave you with this Excerpt from *Make A Difference with the Power of Connection* by Mary Robinson Reynolds:

> *To get what you want,*
> *you must give away what you want.*
> *If you want love, give it away.*
> *If you want respect, give it away.*
> *If you want honesty, give it away.*
> *If you want cooperation, give it away.*
> *If you want compassion, give it away.*
> *If you want control, give it away!*
> *It's really very simple when you think about it.*

I know you'll love putting this into practice. Try doing this at least three times a day every day for the next week, and watch the magic happen! Go ahead, and I'll see you in the next chapter when you're ready.

Chapter Ten

AUTHENTICITY IS THE WAY

Authenticity is a collection of choices that we have to make every day. It's about the choice to show up and be real. The choice to be honest. The choice to let our true selves be seen.

—BRENÉ BROWN, Author, *The Gifts of Imperfection*

THE POLAR OPPOSITE OF TRYING TOO FUCKING HARD IS BEING 100 percent authentic. In fact, the more authentic you are, the less hard you need to try. In fact, you won't have to try hard at all—you'll be living in such a wonderful state of flow you'll find getting what you want to be virtually effortless.

Can you imagine how great it would be to live in a state of almost zero stress? Where your relationships are solid, you have wonderful self-esteem, doing work you love (that doesn't feel like work)? Doing only the things you love, buying only what you need or want, going to places with people who make you feel like a million bucks?

It's possible, and you (yes, you!) can do it!

Why does this work so well? Said simply: authenticity is a magnet. It makes those around us feel comfortable and safe. But for now, let's focus on you and how great you're going to feel!

I've had various opportunities to learn how powerful authenticity can be.

As I mentioned earlier, I was inspired to write the book (and the series) *The Successful Single Mom*. Ultimately, that book changed my life. But not only in the way I described before. It also proved something interesting to me—we connect with others through our authentic stories, and sharing our authentic stories is what connects others to us.

When I wrote *The Successful Single Mom*, I worked with seven single moms to validate my theories and prove my personal findings. Since I didn't consider myself a "real" writer at the time, I figured I'd probably have a dozen readers at most. As a result, I was inspired to write my unabashed truth. I didn't use creative license or censor myself in any way; I simply wrote *my real truth*. My real feelings, the "ugly dirties," as I call them. As it turns out, my authenticity is what made the books wildly popular. Who knew? Well, I didn't!

Had I known I would sell more than a half-million copies total, I can guarantee you I would have toned down my sharing, used some creative license, and left out a few (all!) embarrassing details. But then, would so many women have found my books helpful? Would I have been able to make as big of a difference in the lives of my fellow single moms? I'm gonna vote no on this one.

I won't spend a ton of time here talking about the importance of connection, other than to say again that the number one factor of a long, healthy life has been proven to be a connection with others. When you have strong friendships and relationships, you will live longer and be healthier. Your ticket to a long, healthy, and happy ride is connection.

We know this, if only intuitively, from the moment we're born. If you want to see authenticity in its purest form in action, watch kids, especially young children. Before we send them off to school to be "normalized," they will say what they mean and mean what they say. They are direct and easy with each other (and with us), and honestly delightful. And when we meet an authentic adult, we can't help but love them (even if we don't vibe exactly with all of their authentic parts and pieces).

WHY IS AUTHENTICITY ATTRACTIVE?

Why is authenticity so attractive? Because it touches our authenticity, the part of us that desires to connect with another's authenticity. Somewhere, sometimes very deep inside of us, is a desire to express our authenticity. When we see others express theirs, we feel like we have permission to do so ourselves. And we wonder what life would be like if we did.

Let's go back to kids for a minute. When they start going to school, authenticity takes a backseat to conformity. Being "different" often means becoming a target, and our internal survival skills both help us by providing protection and hinder us because we lose our true selves. It's unfortunate because ultimately, we conform out of our fear of being disliked, rejected, or even bullied. As adults, most of us stick to conforming for our entire lives because we associate ultimate pain with expressing our authentic selves. Sad, right?

Sad but true, and also tragic, because I believe authenticity is our very best asset. Being authentic is honoring yourself at your core, which allows you to give your best self to others and the world. When we conform, we lose out. The world loses out. Lose-lose. No good.

The opposite of living an authentic life is altering one's authentic self to fit in. It's basically doing what someone else is doing. When you do that, at most, you'll be second—because someone is the original and they will win every time.

But how can you give your best when you're trying to adapt and adjust and fit in? Wouldn't it be better to relax into your true self? I say yes!

If you continue to send a conforming representative out into the world, you'll always know something isn't right, and you're not doing the right thing. You're not doing you, and that's a bummer.

HOW ABOUT NOW?

When is the right time to embrace your authentic self and see what good can come from it? How about right this minute? If you need permission, here it is. Go ahead and embrace yourself, close the book, and get on with your day, if you're ready.

Chances are, though, you need to think and process your way into it. Fair enough; it's a scary world out there. I hear you.

Take some time to read and think through your answers to these questions:

- Who are you?
- What do you stand for?
- Why do you do the things you like to do?

Your answers can begin to act as a filter for what you do and what you don't do. What could you start doing that would make you feel happy and joyful? You can create so many wonderful things, situations, and relationships from a place of authenticity. You have so many gifts to share with the world!

You don't have to go all-in right this second. A major change in your main profession might be in order. If it is, great. If not, great. If what makes your heart sing is a side hustle or part-time gig, that's okay, too, as long as you're doing it in some shape or form on the *regular*.

The obvious challenge with being a copy instead of an original is you're indistinguishable from everyone else. Not only will you not stand out, but you also won't measure up to the true original, either. If you're a copy, there's nothing to distinguish you from the masses. There are enough copies out there, my friend, and you were born to stand out.

At a time when people, skills, and services are being commoditized, authenticity is the one thing left that will prevent *you* from being commoditized as well.

Your authentic self is something irreplaceable and not replicable. *There never has been, and never will be, another you.*

Am I getting through? I hope so! You can, should, and must let your light shine!

The very thing that you are suppressing is the very thing that will set you free.

Who is your favorite entertainer? I love Carrie Underwood. I love her because her songs and their lyrics are written with her, for her, by her. She doesn't try to be anyone else, she's embraced herself as a person, woman, artist, and performer.

Like me, can you tell a product of a corporate marketing machine? Those who have their songs and lyrics written for them, in an attempt to create magic, a hit, a star. We almost always can tell whose songs are from the heart, from their authentic selves. We may not know for sure, but we just *know*.

We know it when we hear it, see it, feel it. There is no filter on our phone camera for adjusting or seeing our aura, energy, authenticity. You either let it glow from within, or you don't.

The fear that squashes our authenticity is based in wanting to be liked. It is instilled in us as children because being different meant being a target. Not only that, as an adult, there is an increased pressure to fit in or face major rejection. It can feel like it's better to fit in than stand out, because not fitting in means no job, no living, no relationships. And shit, what if you are authentic and nobody likes you?

I hear you! I'm tall, and from a young age being tall made me a target. Throw in my Dorothy Hamill haircut, low self-esteem, and being a nerd (a band nerd, no less), and I didn't stand a chance! Until I did, because I defaulted to being, and staying authentic.

It's true; throw up your freak flag, and there may be some people who give you the side-eye and keep moving. But I promise you, there will be more folks than not who will be drawn to your authentic self like a moth to a flame.

Why? Because your authenticity stems from the superconscious, the part of the human consciousness we all share. When you express yours, in whatever way feels great to you (such as in your writing, speaking, painting, singing, lecturing, or creating), it's akin to sending up your own personal bat signal. Your PLUs (the "People Like You," from my book *Vision to Reality*) can, and will, see it! And, they will flock to you in droves; they won't be able to help it! They will see and feel in you what they sense in themselves.

How many times have you met someone you feel like you've known forever? Dispensing with the formalities usually associated with making a friend, you discover within minutes or hours of meeting you like the same things, are drawn to the same situations and people, and feel like you've met a long-lost friend.

For a moment, you dropped the pretense and opened yourself up. Something permitted you to do so. Perhaps it was the other person's authenticity, maybe all of the ingredients came together *just so* and allowed the connection to occur. Nevertheless, it happened, and you know to what I refer.

I felt incredibly comfortable with my husband Byron right away. Introduced by a mutual friend, our first conversation was comfortable. Our first date lasted hours; we never ran out of things to talk about. On our second date, I felt drawn to him and relaxed. Suffice it to say, my history did not lend itself to me showing up in any relationship with buckets full of trust.

To this day, Byron is the most authentic person I know. It is common for my friends and clients to become his friends and clients. In fact, on more than a dozen occasions, I've called someone, asked what they were doing, only to hear, *I'm about to have lunch with your husband!* He's that cool.

Here's why we connected: before meeting him, I had decided I was done trying to twist myself into a pretzel to be with someone, as a friend or in a relationship. I stood grounded in the knowledge I am a kind and honest person. I would just be myself and see how it turned out.

I had long been trying too fucking hard, and it was exhausting.

Pretending I wasn't cold, hungry, or tired was exhausting. Pretending I was excited to do things when I wasn't? Also exhausting.

So, I decided to be okay with me, and okay with others, and roll along.

When Byron asked me out, he suggested we visit what was, at the time, the new Town Square in Las Vegas. Years before, I had dated a guy who loved me in short skirts and high heels and insisted I wear them (with no regard to the weather or my comfort). Well, it was December in Las Vegas, and although it wasn't Minnesota and twenty-six degrees outside, it was cold *to me* nevertheless. I said, "I'll be wearing jeans, boots, and a long coat." I mentioned this for two reasons, one, we were meeting on a blind date, and two, I wanted to hear his reaction. Always a comedian, he said, "That's what I'll be wearing, too."

Turns out being my authentic self landed me the best guy ever. If I had tried to be anyone other than myself, I know for sure Byron would've turned heel and run. Without reservation, without looking back. As an authentic person, he abhors inauthenticity (as do I).

Deciding to be my authentic self was the best decision I've ever made. It just might be one of yours, too.

IT'S YOUR TURN TO AUTHENTICATE

If you've spent a season or a lifetime hiding your true self from others, I encourage you to stop trying so fucking hard and just be your authentic self.

If you've fallen into the trap of becoming almost a different person depending upon where or who you're with, throw on your authenticity cape and get out there!

Why? Because the rewards are too good to pass up!

WHY YOU SHOULD TAKE A RISK AND BE AUTHENTIC

It is a risk to stop being inauthentic and start being your real self. There is a chance you will experience some serious change in your life. Some of your friends may choose to leave, just as you bring new ones into your life. You may discover relationships you thought were lifelong will expand, contract, or dissolve completely.

You may realize you spent several years and hundreds of thousands of dollars to get an education to engage in a profession you dread every day.

I would be remiss if I didn't mention there is some legitimate pain involved in making significant changes in your life, and without question, upping your authenticity could be a major change. You and your life will sort itself out. You will be okay—dare I say better—by becoming your authentic self.

Lowering your defenses and upping your authenticity will leave its mark on everything you do: work, play, people, and situations. It will touch every aspect of your life from your social life to your environment, even the smallest action you take. It will affect others and allow you to be connected to them, in ways you may not have experienced until now.

When you do, life will feel right and better. Just like it's the life you were supposed to be living this whole time. You won't care about what others think, or what others might be expecting of you. You'll feel comfortable cruising on your own path.

As a result, you'll achieve success as you define it. You'll have more than enough of everything you need (including money, nourishment, love, goods, opportunities, and more) right when you need them.

You'll stop relying on what others think of you and begin to care deeply about what you think of you. With any luck, you'll not only stop judging yourself and start loving yourself in a new and wonderful way. You'll be able to heal your past hurts, forgive anyone who needs forgiving, and let go of your "shoulds."

You will live authentically because it feels good. When you deliver your true self to others you sleep well at night, knowing that you're honoring yourself—and you're the only you that will ever exist in the universe! I mean, you don't want to waste your precious chance to let your light shine as bright as it can possibly shine!

HOW TO BECOME MORE AUTHENTIC

If you've conformed your sweet little ass off for decades, eliminating any inauthenticity will be an adjustment for sure.

Now you know why, but you might not be clear on the how (other than what I've already covered in this book). Yes, each of the previous chapters in this book touches on how to honor your authentic self. But here are some tried-and-true ways to live authentically now:

LISTEN TO YOUR POSITIVE INNER VOICE (AND TURN THAT SUCKER UP!).

My daughter is learning to drive, and when I ask her how she's doing, she confidently says, *I've got this!* She started saying that on her own, probably after hearing me say *I've got this!* lots of times over the past eighteen years. I love she uses that as her mantra!

Turn down your critical inner voice and turn up your positive (and very wise) inner voice. The voice that says we're not enough or we're too much needs to be turned down so low you don't even know it's there (using the mute button is also fine). Our positive inner voice, one that boosts our confidence and reinforces our confidence—is the one to turn *way up* and listen to it on automatic repeat.

If it's been awhile since you've heard it, feel free to call your closest positive friend and ask them to describe you in five positive words.

Next level: write out your vision and some positive affirmations and record yourself saying them. Listen to your recording every day, with some great music as your soundtrack.

MY AUTHENTICITY EXPERIMENT

I decided to experiment with authenticity—on Facebook of course, which is quite possibly a hotbed of inauthenticity. I posted:

> *I'm working on my next book. Assuming you're a positive person in a positive mood, would you please share the 5 most positive words you'd use to describe me?*
>
> *Bonus points if you send the 5 positive words you'd use to describe your closest friends and you post those words in the comments, too (be sure to send them to your friends and ask for their words for you!). You'll help me with my book AND make your friends' day.*
>
> *Thanks in advance!*

Of course, my husband commented right away. He said: *optimistic, strong, honest, intellectual,* and *loyal.* I had no idea those would be his words for me. I got to give him my words for him. We had a moment. It was awesome! I highly encourage you to do this with your family and friends.

If you're either (a) having trouble coming up with your five words, or (b) you don't think you have any, copy and edit the above text and send it to your closest friends (or post it on Facebook). I, for one, would love to see more positivity between people declared publicly.

You at your most authentic has attracted, and kept, those closest to you. My Facebook experiment was fun because it was a great experience to see how others perceive me and to see the words used most often, and I know you'll feel incredible when your nearest and dearest honor you with their words.

SAY YES AND NO.

Make a list of your priorities and all of the things you've "always wanted to do." Are the things you want in life—your deepest priorities and dreams—on your calendar? If not, there are changes you will want to make.

You will have to say *yes* to what you claim is important, and *no* to things you realize don't move the needle for you one way or another.

For example, I have wanted to learn French— to become fluent and be able to speak it as I speak English—for as long as I can remember. I'd dabbled on occasion with apps and even an online course. I bought a workbook and tried my hand at a learn-it-yourself CD program. It wasn't until I made a genuine commitment to study for an hour every day that I started to make progress. I'm not there yet, but I study every day, and I have a French coach I work with once a week.

I have said *no* to watching mindless television and *yes!* to my vision of being a French speaker. Everything on your list, if it is a priority, you will put it onto your calendar. It is that simple.

Identify something you want to do, and then identify pockets of time you could use differently. Track your downtime. If you notice that hours of downtime are being lost to social media or channel surfing, redirect. Train yourself to work on your desired outcome instead. Before you know it, you'll have made measurable progress on something that matters deeply to you.

NEITHER GIVE NOR RECEIVE BULLSHIT.

I'm known for saying, "Don't be coming at me with no bullshit!" As I am a firm believer that what I put out comes back to me multiplied, I also don't go at anyone with any bullshit, either!

If you adopt a No Bullshit policy, your authenticity levels will increase in an accelerated manner. Right before your eyes.

PAY ATTENTION TO HOW YOU FEEL.

You might *think* you're doing all the right things to live authentically. But if you're paying close attention, you may have the feeling you're just not. Stay open to the world around you and the feedback you're getting, not only from the people around you but by the experiences the universe sends your way. Some messages are hard to hear, and some truth is hard to swallow. If you're feeling frustrated, angry, or ill-at-ease, there's a message in there that will help you.

Do more of what makes you feel good and minimize or completely stop the things that make you feel bad.

I've taken some heat for not drinking, going to bed early, and being fifty shades of boring. Alcohol makes me feel awful for days after I drink it, and I have never liked its bitter taste. It was a great day when I discovered virgin piña coladas were even more delicious than their alcohol-laden cousins. I like to turn in early with the "blue hairs" and rise before the sun—it's quiet, I can meditate, read, journal, and write a few thousand words before the rest of the world wakes up. By the time most people are finishing their first cup of coffee, I've finished a workout, and I'm ready for the day (whether I do anything else productive that day or not). I don't work evenings, weekends, or holidays, and if there's a holiday anywhere in the world, I observe it. I'm not instantly responsive on email or texting, but I'm pretty sure there's no colleague, client, or contact who feels like I'm unresponsive.

I am also happy, have almost no stress, and I'm productive by anyone's standards. Why? Because I stopped trying so fucking hard to do things the way others wanted me to do them and figured out how to do them in a way that worked best for me and allowed me to be at my best.

You can do the same thing.

SEEK PROFESSIONAL HELP.

There's a bit of a stigma around that statement. I could hear an echo around the words "professional help" as I wrote them. We trust medical professionals of all kinds, and our mental health should be no different. If you've "got issues" (and who doesn't?), working on treating them with a professional is just the smart play!

A good therapist or even psychiatrist can help you cut through your bullshit, and help you see, as though donning a pair of glasses with the right prescription, in record time. Especially if you have relationships where you question your sanity, you'll be able to find out quickly who you have in your life that is supporting you (and who isn't so much).

Extra cool bonus benefit: A professional doesn't have the emotional involvement of a friend. They are paid to help you identify your truth, own your greatness, and put a plan in place to process pain, past hurts, heal, and move forward.

To find the right person for you, ask for recommendations. Or consult an online service. You may have to visit with a couple of people before you find the right fit. Stay at it! The right mental health professional can help you get your mental health on the right track.

LEARN TO ACCEPT YOURSELF, JUST AS YOU ARE (EVEN AS YOU WORK TO IMPROVE).

Please, as quickly as humanly possible, accept who you are: become body- mind-, and spirit-positive, and practice the love, compassion, and forgiveness you so readily give to others *with yourself.* You won't be any happier when you lose twenty pounds or run that marathon or write that book or get the promotion you want or have the next child (even if you think you will), so just be happy now. In other words, you'll be happy the minute you decide to be happy and stop chasing a set of circumstances rather than loving your life as it is right now.

Pretend you are your own best friend (you are, though, aren't you?) and you've just called for some words of love and encouragement. Say to yourself what you'd say to your best friend. Say what you'd say if your friend were down in the dumps and feeling sad. Say what you'd say if your friend made a mistake and was feeling full of regret. Say what you'd say if your friend just accomplished something amazing and were feeling pretty proud of herself.

Give to yourself what you'd give to *anyone else but yourself* in the reverse situation.

MEDITATE EVERY DAY, EVEN IF IT'S ONLY FOR FIVE MINUTES.

To be your authentic, *nice* self may require some extra self-care. My husband is always up in my grill to "shut down your computer, give it a chance to rest and reboot." He's told me why it's a good idea, and I don't exactly remember (and I'm not going to ask again either, because then I'll be outed for not listening carefully). But I know it's good for my computer to get a break, and isn't your brain (and soul and spirit) worthy of the same extra-special treatment?

Before you demand another day of work from it, give your brain a chance to function at its highest level by shutting it down.

One of the fastest ways to raise up your authentic self while virtually shutting down your need to try too fucking hard is to become quiet. Turn off everything: the radio, television, computer. Any noise makers need some muting. You'll be able to tap into your inner knowing and turn the volume up.

When my meditation game is strong, I not only get intuitive hits and messages from within, I get 'em loud and clear. I get a lot of *do this* and *by all means, Honorée Corder, don't do that! Go here* and *go there instead* messages.

Our recent move was promoted by an intuitive hit I got during a brief phone call with my husband. When I got Hal's message about writing a book together, my first thought was *I'm done writing single mom books.* But my inner voice said, *Have a conversation!* Those are just two of the messages I know I wouldn't have been able to hear if I wasn't quiet enough to hear them.

BENEFITS AND MORE BENEFITS

When you live authentically, you'll not only learn how to be so happy you can hardly stand it, there are a few other cool benefits, too:

You'll be happier and more relaxed. Wherever you'll go, there you'll be. And you'll be darn happy about it.

You'll have better and closer relationships. There are lots of people *just like you* who have the same interests and pursuits. You're going to bond like two peas in a pod when you find other folks who share your curiosities.

You'll be more confident and attractive. I know I've covered this somewhat in depth, but it bears mentioning again. An authentic person is naturally more self-confident, and self-confidence is at the top of the "what makes someone irresistible" list.

You'll have more energy. Pretending to be someone you're not is, frankly, exhausting. When you are who you are, you won't have a strain or drain of your energy. Side benefit: you'll be more creative and productive.

Your ability to read people accurately will spike. Spotting the authentic from the fake will be easy. You'll be able to tell when someone is trying to fit in. Those you meet along the way may not be trying to deceive or be inauthentic—in fact, their inauthenticity may be what's comfortable to them. They've been trying to fit in for so long, they aren't sure what it would be like to be authentic. But you'll be able to spot them from a mile away and steer clear or at least limit your exposure.

By the way: turning on your light of authenticity will permit others to turn theirs on. You may be the person who allows others to own their authenticity.

Finally, everyone else is already taken. Stop trying so fucking hard and be your authentic, unusual, and beautiful true self.

Today you are you! That is truer than true!
There is no one alive who is you-er than you!

–DR. SEUSS

YOUR TIME IS NOW!

My intention for this book was to give you the inspiration and tools you need to live the very life you are here to live—one that up until now, was only a picture in your wildest imagination.

Just as Rome wasn't built in a day, it may take some time for you to peel back some layers and reveal your core to the world. You may not be able to just stop trying so hard in an instant, and that's perfectly fine. You're on your journey, and your timing is yours and yours alone.

If I may suggest one additional thing: in whatever way feels best, start today. Don't wait any longer to unveil at least some parts of yourself to some people in your life. As you see others accept you as you are, applaud your courage, and jump on your bandwagon, you'll begin to feel more and more comfortable revealing your true self not only to yourself but also to the world.

My best wishes and blessings for you and what's to come.

AUTHOR NOTES

WELCOME TO MY AUTHOR NOTES. THIS IS WHERE I REFLECT back on this book and share my thoughts about it. This section isn't edited or censored, just 100 percent Honorée right up in here. Author Notes are inspired by my fellow author and dear friend, Julie Huss, who based a character on me in one of her books. (I mentioned her early in this book, she writes incredibly popular naughty romance novels.)

Julie and I met at an author conference, and our observation that *most people are just trying too fucking hard* combined with our authentic personalities drew us together. We're both known for our authenticity and keen dislike and distrust of those who *aren't*.

While I was writing this book, I was experiencing a whole lotta people who are just trying too fucking hard. Posting up several different book covers on Facebook and asking the GP (general public), which one *they* liked best.

First of all, the GP doesn't know what a good book cover looks like. Does traditional publishing share different covers for approval? No fucking way—because unless you have an eye for it, you don't even know what you're looking at or for. Movie studios don't release several different versions of movies, nor do they engage amateurs to produce a professional product. I could go on and on, but I'm pretty sure you get my point.

But lest you think I'm just sitting here on my very comfortable sofa judging the entire world, *I am not.*

For far too long, I tried far too fucking hard. I wanted to please people so they would like me. As it turns out, these were the same people who ultimately didn't give a rat's ass about me. While I was trying too fucking hard to please the wrong people, I was simultaneously pushing away really good people who cared deeply. And as I navigated losing friends, the end of a marriage, and loads of therapy, I came to terms with the common denominator in every situation: me.

I was trying too fucking hard and I was exhausted. I realized I had an innate desire to be happy. So, I exhaled, took a step back, and then several more as I did exactly what I advised you to do in the final chapter. I got a therapist, started listening more to myself than to others, said no a lot more than I said yes, and got busy doing pretty much only what I wanted to do—the things that made me happy.

When I was growing up, my mom used to say, *Bless her heart.* She would say that mostly when someone was going through a rough time, and she meant it in the purest, most beautiful way.

In the South, *Bless her heart* has more of a condescending judgment about it. Like, *Bless her heart, she doesn't know any better.*

I got to the point where I saw so many people trying too fucking hard, I was saying *Bless their hearts!* And I was anything but loving and supportive. But as I always am, I was working on myself when I had a realization. In an instant, I understood why I don't suffer from anxiety or depression, I am really enjoying life, and while I have a rather small group of friends, I have some incredible humans in my life. *Because I wasn't trying too fucking hard, in fact, quite the opposite.*

And I developed a mission to help others live a happy and wonderful life as well. So here we are. And I'm at the end of this leg of the journey. I feel like I've shared what I know and hope it's enough. What do you think? I'd love to hear. Send me an email, if you're so inclined, and let me know what you think.

Honoree@HonoreeCorder.com

With gratitude,

HC

QUICK FAVOR

I'M WONDERING, DID YOU ENJOY THIS BOOK?

First of all, thank you for reading my book! May I ask a quick favor?

Will you take a moment to leave an honest review for this book on Amazon? Reviews are the BEST way to help others purchase the book.

You can go to the link below and write your thoughts. I appreciate you!

HONOREECORDER.COM/STOPTRYINGREVIEW

GRATITUDE

To my husband, partner, and best friend, Byron. Thank you for being an example of authenticity and loving me at my most authentic.

To my daughter and inspiration, Lexi, I'm so grateful to be your mom. You're an example of kindness and authenticity every day, and I'm so proud of you.

To my bonus daughter, Tiffany, welcome to the family.

To Christina, you're just the greatest. Your authentic self is pretty amazing!

To my book team: So much love and gratitude to Alyssa Archer, for being an incredible editor and brilliant mind; Jackie Dana for proofreading and sweet notes; Dino Marino for once again knocking my cover design out of the park, and Christina at 3CsBooks for your gorgeous interior design work. Y'all make me look so good!

WHO IS HONORÉE?

Honorée Corder is the author of dozens of books, including: *You Must Write a Book; I Must Write My Book; The Nifty 15: Write Your Book in Just 15 Minutes a Day!; The Prosperous Writers* book series; *Vision to Reality: How Short Term Massive Action Equals Long Term Maximum Results; Business Dating: Applying Relationship Rules in Business for Ultimate Success; The Successful Single Mom* book series; *If Divorce is a Game, These are the Rules*; and *The Divorced Phoenix.*

She is also Hal Elrod's business partner in *The Miracle Morning* book series, and together they've published fourteen titles to date. Honorée coaches business professionals, writers, and aspiring non-fiction authors who want to publish their books to bestseller status, create a platform, and develop multiple streams of income. She also does all sorts of other magical things, and her badassery is legendary. You can find out more at HonoreeCorder.com.

Honorée Enterprises, Inc.
Honoree@HonoreeCorder.com
http://www.HonoreeCorder.com
Twitter & Instagram: @Honoree
Facebook: http://www.facebook.com/Honoree

BOOK HONORÉE TO SPEAK

Honorée—you got me fired up! Thank you for building my confidence! Honorée's presentation was the perfect kick-off and her message of visualizing success was spot-on.
  ~Johnny B Truant, COO Sterling Stone

Honorée really captured the attention of our tribe, which is no easy task. Her quick-witted take on the world had them riveted—and keep in mind she followed Brooke Shields. Her stories are real, completely relatable, and just the sort of motivation women need to bring out their best.
  ~India Hicks, Founder, India Hicks Inc.

If you want engaging, results-oriented content without any fluff, I highly recommend booking Honorée Corder to speak at your event.
  ~Hal Elrod, Best-selling Author,
  The Miracle Morning

Honorée Corder is THE self-publishing expert, but that's not all. For almost 20 years she's inspired and guided professionals to double their income and triple their time off. Her genuine charm and expert knowledge are guaranteed to help your audience, business, or group achieve the success they desire, all while laughing along the way.

Book Honorée as your Keynote Speaker and you're guaranteed to make your event highly energizing and valuable!

For more information visit www.HonoreeCorder.com/speaking

Made in the USA
Columbia, SC
24 August 2018